simply chilis, chowders, and stews

simply chilis, chowders, and stews

Carol Heding Munson

SURREY BOOKS

Chicago

SIMPLY CHILIS, CHOWDERS, AND STEWS
is published by Surrey Books, Inc.
230 E. Ohio St., Suite 120, Chicago, IL 60611

First Edition 1 2 3 4 5

This book is manufactured in the United States of America

Library of Congress Cataloging-in-Publication Data

Munson, Carol

    Simply chilis, chowders, and stews / by Carol Heding Munson—1st ed.
    p.   cm.
    Includes index.
    ISBN 1-57284-015-3 (pbk.)
    1. Soups. 2. Stews. 3. Chili con carne. 4. Low calorie diet.—Recipes.
    5. Low-Fat diet—Recipes. 6. Low-cholesterol diet—Recipes.
    7. Salt-free diet—Recipes. I. Title.
    TX757.M86   1998
    641.8'23—dc21   97-44380
                               CIP

Illustrations ©1998 Patti Green
Editorial and production: Bookcrafters, Inc., Chicago
Design and Typesetting: Joan Sommers Design, Chicago

For free Catalog and prices on quantity purchases, contact Surrey Books at the
address above

This title is distributed to the trade by Publishers Group West

A hearty thank you to Russell and Roger, who sampled and critiqued every recipe and enthusiastically offered opinions. And a loving thank you to Lowell for his generous contribution of recipes, his cheerful handling of the daily supermarket shuttle, and his invaluable assistance with recipe testing. His encouragement and support made this book possible.

contents

introduction

It happens every time the temperature drops below 60°: My busy-hour meal plans become a potpourri of chilis, chowders, and stews. And with good reason. They're hearty. They're comforting. They're easy to make—just as easy as grilling a burger and tossing together a simple salad. And most are quick to cook—quick enough to have dinner ready to eat in 45 minutes or less, including prep time. What's more, chilis, chowders, and stews have what it takes to chase the chills on a brisk day: A steaming hot broth.

But that's not all. Chilis, chowders, and stews are carefree concoctions just brimming with classic ingredients: Tender lean poultry, meat, and seafood; nutty-tasting pasta and rice; and fresh vegetables—the kind of basics that have plenty of irresistible palate appeal. I love those basics because they not only taste great but they're readily available in an average well-stocked supermarket, so shopping's a breeze.

Another reason chilis, chowders, and stews, like the ones in this book, make it big in my meal plans: They're perfect for today's dietwise lifestyles. They offer tons of old-fashioned flavor in up-to-date family favorites—not excess fat, sodium, and calories as you might find in your supermarket's fast-food/deli aisle. Said simply: Chilis, chowders, and stews make for wonderfully satisfying, wonderfully delicious *complete* meals.

Why did I write this book? To share the fast-to-fix dishes that win rave reviews with my family and friends. But don't just take my word for simple, easy, tasty. Sample and enjoy *Monkfish-Cheddar Chowder, Shrimp and Sausage Gumbo, Meatball and Corkscrew Pasta Stew, New England Boiled Dinner, Moroccan Chicken Stew with Couscous, Lightning-Fast Chili,* or *Mesquite Chicken Chili,* to name a few. Prefer something vegetarian? Then give *Black Magic Garlic Chowder, Cheese Ravioli with Basil,* or *French Vegetable Chowder with Pistou* a shot.

Once you've tried chilis, chowders, and stews, I think they'll become a delightful part of your personal recipe collection, too.

secrets to making super chilis, chowders, and stews

Looking for recipes with "simple," "splendid," and "sure-fire success" written all over them? Then you've come to the right place because chilis, chowders, and stews meet those criteria, and then some. I'll explain:

They're 1-2-3 easy to make—no elaborate, lengthy directions to follow. Basically, all you do is toss everything into a pot, then simmer the mixture a bit. It's ready to eat when the food's tender and the flavors have blended. But there are variations. To achieve different tastes and textures, some chilis, chowders, and stews call for quick sautéing and even some pureeing, two simple steps done in a flash.

They've got tons of flavor. This is why: As they cook, vegetables, meats, seafood, and grains soak up the sophisticated flavors of herbs, spices, and other seasonings. But the flavorings needn't be unique or exotic; a little minced basil or garlic or freshly ground black pepper can add unforgettable character. Later in this chapter, I'll talk more about seasonings.

They're fail-proof. In other words, chilis, chowders, and stews are never fussy and are always forgiving. For example: Prefer more carrots in your stew? Or how about less spinach? Maybe an additional chicken breast half? Go ahead; make the change or changes. And if you need to fudge the cooking time because the phone rang, relax about it and do so. Your stew will still taste great.

If you're new to chili-, chowder-, and stew-making, be sure to check out the rest of this chapter. It contains helpful information about equipment, seasonings, garnishes, storing, and reheating.

EQUIPMENT

Now that you're ready to whip up a fast and fabulous chili, chowder, or stew, what kind of equipment will you need? Only a few basic kitchen tools—none of which is specialized or high-tech. These are some of the items I find useful:

Cutting board. It matters little whether you select a wooden or plastic board. Just be sure to get one that's small enough for easy washing and large enough for unhindered chopping. I like a 10 x 14-inch board. For food-safety sake, remember to wash the board thoroughly after each use.

Chef's knife. This is a must-have item that'll put your food preparation on the fast-track. It's handy for cutting meats, chopping vegetables, mincing garlic and herbs. An 8-inch chef's knife gets my vote for versatility, although some cooks prefer the 6- or 10-inch variety.

Paring knife. With its short blade, 3 or 4 inches long, a paring knife will make quick work of trimming mushrooms, peeling apples and garlic, and other similar tasks. I like the 3-inch size, finding it easiest to manipulate.

Vegetable peeler. This simple tool is another can't-do-without. It's ideal for peeling thin-skinned root vegetables like carrots, potatoes, and parsnips. For no-bother peeling, be sure to get a peeler with a swivel blade that's sharp.

Wooden spoons. These aren't a necessity, but I prefer them over metal and plastic varieties for stirring and mixing tasks. Why? They don't scratch pots and pans and don't become stained. The handles don't get hot, and they don't melt even if you accidentally leave them touching a hot pot. And their shallow bowls are well suited to stirring. Medium-length handles are most versatile.

Immersion blender. I didn't own one of these gadgets until recently. But now I can't cook without it. If you don't have one, you'll need a potato masher, blender, food processor, or food mill to puree the ingredients for several of the thick and creamy chowders and stews in this book. Make sure your immersion blender is designed for pureeing hot foods.

Large spoon or ladle. Either is perfect for dishing out a steaming chili, chowder, or stew.

4-quart pot. What makes a pot a pot and not a saucepan? Size, 4 quarts or larger, and two handles. Most of the recipes in this book fill a 4-quart pot half to two-thirds full, a depth that allows room for stirring and simmering. If you're purchasing a pot, look for a quality, heavy nonstick one with a snug-fitting lid.

Spice grinder or mortar and pestle. These reasonably priced and easy-to-find tools didn't appear in my kitchen until about 5 years ago, and even then they came as gifts. Very welcome ones, I might add. Get one or the other only if you'd like to grind your own spices, a practice I recommend because freshly ground seasonings have more punch than preground varieties. (See "Seasonings," p. xiii.)

Slow cooker. Consisting of a crockery liner and a surrounding metal heating unit, this relatively inexpensive, small electric appliance allows you to simmer food unattended for hours. It's best suited to recipes containing meats, poultry, and sturdy vegetables, such as carrots and potatoes, that can withstand lengthy cooking. But you can get away with cooking tender vegetables, such as peas and broccoli florets, and pasta if you add them during the last hour of simmering. Though a slow cooker is optional for chili-, chowder-, and stew-making, I've given slow-cooking directions for many of the recipes in this book (see "Helpful Hints" under individual recipes). You'll need a 4-quart cooker. Be aware that slow-cooked dishes have a slightly different texture and flavor from quick-cooked versions.

Pressure cooker. For meals in minutes, you can't beat using a pressure cooker, which cooks foods at 220°. No, that's not a typo. Pressure cookers are designed with heavy pots, special locking lids, and pressure regulators to raise the internal cooking temperature higher than the boiling point of water. Though expensive, they're terrific for cooking meats, poultry, and sturdy vegetables—carrots, potatoes, squash, beets, and such-in short order, sometimes in as little as 1 to 5 minutes.

But cooking under pressure does have its quirks: Foods that foam during cooking (split peas, lentils, pasta, rice, apples, and cranberries, for example) are no-nos because they can clog the pressure regulator. Many cookers require at least 1 cup of liquid. Without the fluid, they can't generate the steam necessary to build pressure. Quick-cooking, delicate vegetables need special handling to halt cooking at the crisp-tender stage. And textures and flavors differ from those of conventionally cooked foods. My recommendations: To get the most from a pressure cooker, check out some of the excellent pressure cooker cookbooks on the market. Always follow the instructions included with your cooker. And if you're purchasing a new cooker, consider getting nothing smaller than a 6-quart.

As with the slow cooker, a pressure cooker is optional for chili-, chowder-, and stew-making. I have, however, given pressure cooking directions in several recipes under "Helpful Hints."

Microwave. Can you simmer chilis, chowders, and stews in a microwave? Absolutely. And you can achieve very good results. But please note that the recipes in this book were created using stove-top techniques. If you plan to use your microwave, here are some guidelines for adapting conventional recipes:

- Cut food into small, uniform pieces so they cook evenly.
- Whenever a recipe calls for sautéing, brown the food in a skillet, then transfer it to a microwave-safe dish.
- Cook chilis, chowders, and stews in a microwave dish that's covered with waxed paper, a lid, or vented plastic wrap.
- Turn the dish or stir it every 2 to 3 minutes, or as recommended in your microwave manual.
- Cook on Medium-High or High, and check for doneness after about 10 minutes. Thereafter, check food approximately every 30 seconds so it doesn't become overcooked.

SEASONINGS

Like the equipment needed for stirring up a chili, chowder, or stew, the herbs and spices called for are familiar and readily available. There's no need to traipse to specialty markets or to peruse mail-order catalogs, both of which can take precious time. Everything you need should be in your well-stocked, local supermarket. Even exotic-sounding blends, such as Szechuan seasoning and herbes de Provence, are now available on the shelf with name-brand spices.

Since early times, man has gone to the ends of the earth to obtain herbs and spices. And for good cause. Herbs and spices give foods pizzazz, signature flavors, special character. They also impart uniqueness and depth of flavor. Imagine Hungarian goulash without paprika. Tacos sans cumin. Italian sausage minus fennel. The results would be remarkably routine and decidedly dull dishes, agreed?

To get the most from nature's flavor enhancers, buy herbs and spices in small quantities, meaning the smallest jars you can find, and replace them often. How often is often? Certainly, any dried herb (and many spices) more than a year old has lost much of its flavor power and is ready for retirement. Stash dried herbs and spices in a cool, dry, dark spot. Before using dried herbs, crush them between your fingers to release their fragrance and flavor.

And fresh herbs? Their heavenly scent and flavor surpasses that of the dried variety, hands down. So, I urge you to choose fresh, whenever you can. Store herbs in plastic bags in your refrigerator and use them within several days.

As for spices, I suggest getting whole ones. They must be grated or ground before use, true, but freshly ground spices have greater impact than preground varieties, which invariably lose flavor during storage.

For top-notch flavor, add spices, which are the pungent roots, barks, stems, buds, fruits, and leaves of tropical or subtropical plants, near the beginning of cooking. This is especially true when you're making chilis, chowders, and stews, dishes that require more than a minute or two of simmering. The reason: The concentrated, robust flavors of most spices, with the exceptions of black and white pepper, benefit from cooking.

Herbs, however, are the delicate leaves of plants that grow in temperate climes. And their light flavor easily dissipates in heat. Therefore, my herbal rule of thumb: Add herbs near the end of cooking. Exceptions to the rule include rosemary and thyme—two rather intensely flavored herbs.

It may never happen, but what to do if you accidentally overseason a chili, chowder, or stew? You can try the following rescues:

- Simmer a peeled, quartered raw potato in the mixture for 10 to 15 minutes. It'll soak up some of the over-exuberant spicing. Discard the potato pieces.
- Use a slotted spoon to remove as much of the spice as possible.
- Stir in a teaspoon of sugar.
- Prepare a second batch without seasonings. Combine the two batches.

Though technically not a seasoning, a flavorful stock or broth also has a tremendous influence on the taste of a chili, chowder, or stew. In the recipes here, feel free to use a homemade stock, seasoned canned broth, or undoctored canned broth. Any of them will give your dish a subtle flavor base.

For descriptions of several herbs and spices, see the Glossary (p. 127). For a list of herbs and spices and the foods that they complement, see "Using herbs and Spices" (p. 136).

GARNISHES

All too often, garnishes are the part of the recipe we ignore. I don't know why. Perhaps it's because they seem to be optional, a fancy extra. Not so. Garnishes can enliven a dish, making both its flavor and color practically pop off the plate. These are some of the garnishes that work beautifully with chilis, chowders, and stews:

Bacon, crumbled

Basil, fresh: whole or snipped leaves

Caraway seeds

Cheese, grated or shredded

Chives, snipped

Cilantro, fresh: whole or snipped leaves

Croutons, plain or garlic

Paprika, sprinkled

Parsley, fresh: whole or snipped leaves

Scallions, bias-sliced

Sour cream, swirled

QUICK COOKING

Simply said, putting together a chili, chowder, or stew is a breeze, almost a no-brainer. But when you're rush-hour frazzled even simple, routine kitchen tasks take forever (or at least they seem to). But it needn't be that way. Here are four steps that can help put preparation on the fast-track:

Step 1. Set the table. Set out silverware, plates, cups, and serving dishes before starting any preparation or cooking.

Step 2. Organize your thoughts. Begin by reading the recipe from start to finish.

Step 3. Gather required ingredients, and place them within fingertip reach. Start pasta cooking water since it takes several minutes to come to a boil.

Step 4. Prepare the ingredients. That is, do all the slicing, dicing, and measuring and put the prepared ingredients into small bowls and cups or into piles on waxed paper before cooking. When chopping and slicing, cut the dry ingredients, such as bread, first. Then you can cut moist ones, such as onions, without having to wash the cutting board or food-processor bowl. Return extra ingredients to the pantry, fridge, or freezer.

BONUS BATCHES

If your culinary mindset is anything like mine, you consider leftovers (or double batches) as bonus meals or quick heat 'n' eat meals—a godsend when the time squeeze is *really* on. And most chilis, chowders, and stews store beautifully for another time. But not all. These are the ones requiring special handling:

Anything containing pasta and lots of yummy broth. During refrigeration or freezing, the pasta continues to absorb liquid and oversoften. When it's reheated the results are soggy, not al dente, pasta. A fix is easy: Simply add the pasta to each batch when you're ready to serve it.

Chowders and stews with potatoes. These dishes will keep in the refrigerator for a day or two. But potatoes don't freeze well. Either add cooked potatoes at the last minute or eliminate them from the recipe.

Chowders made with milk. These dishes will be all right in the refrigerator until the next day, but don't keep them longer. Reheat them very carefully, taking care not to boil the milk or it may curdle. If you must freeze them, reserve the milk, and add it when reheating the chowder.

Dishes containing avocado. This vegetable darkens rapidly when the flesh is cut and exposed to air. Add avocado right before serving the dish.

Remember, when storing extra portions to refrigerate or freeze them as soon as possible. Food safety experts recommend chilling foods within 2 hours of cooking. I try for even less time—no more than an hour. Use refrigerated chilis, chowders, and stews within 2 days and frozen dishes within 2 weeks.

To reheat a chili, chowder, or stew, thaw it either in the refrigerator or microwave. Then, reheat it on the stove top or in the microwave until it's bubbly hot throughout.

NUTRITIONAL INFORMATION

For the readers keeping an eye on calories, grams of fat, and milligrams of sodium, I've included a nutritional analysis of each recipe in this book. The analyses were calculated using Nutritionist IV by First Data Bank. Please remember that all such analyses are close approximations. To get exact analyses, you'd have to send *your* dinners, each one of them, to a laboratory for complete chemical breakdowns!

This is what to keep in mind as you read the nutritional information: Each analysis was figured for a single serving. If you eat a larger or smaller portion, you'll be taking in proportionally more or less calories, fat, carbohydrates, sodium, and fiber. Garnishes and optional ingredients were not included in the analyses, and, in most cases, would not have much impact on nutritional statistics. If an alternate ingredient is given or a range of amounts appears, the analysis was figured on the first item or smallest amount.

Refer often to the nutritional analyses that accompany the recipes. They'll help you—just as the "Nutritional Facts" labels on packages do—plan and prepare tasty meals that are good for you and that you and your family or soulmates will love.

fast and flavorful stocks

Beef Broth with Spice

Beef Stock

Chicken Stock

Quick Sage Chicken Broth

Vegetable Stock

BEEF BROTH WITH SPICE

When you want a spicy broth, give this easy version a try. It's just what the broth-meister ordered for perking up a bland dish!

1 can (14 ounces) fat-free beef broth
1 medium onion, quartered
1 clove garlic
1 tablespoon dry red wine
1 teaspoon pickling spice

Combine broth, onion, garlic, and wine in a 2-quart saucepan. Place pickling spice in a mesh tea bag or tie it in cheesecloth. Cover pot, and bring broth to a boil. Reduce heat; simmer broth for 10 minutes. Discard vegetables and seasonings.

PREPARATION TIME:
5 minutes
COOKING TIME:
10 minutes
YIELD: **about 2 cups**

PER CUP:
Calories: 57
Fat (g): 0.1
Saturated Fat (g): 0
Cholesterol (mg): 0
Carbohydrates (g): 3.4
Sodium (mg): 136
Dietary Fiber (g): 0

BEEF STOCK

A flavorful stock that's easy to prepare in either a stock pot or a pressure cooker.

PREPARATION TIME:
15 minutes
COOKING TIME:
2 hours
YIELD: *about 9 cups*

10 cups water
2 ribs from roasted beef rib roast
2 celery stalks, leaves included, halved
4 large onions, with skins, quartered
4 medium carrots, halved
1 parsnip, halved
2 bay leaves
8 whole black peppercorns
1 sprig parsley
5 sage leaves

Combine water, beef, celery, onions, carrots, parsnips, bay leaves, peppercorns, parsley, and sage in an 8-quart pot. Cover pot, and bring stock to a boil. Reduce heat; simmer stock for 2 hours.

Line a colander with cheesecloth. Pour stock through colander into a large bowl or pot. Discard bones, vegetables, and seasonings. Chill stock, then skim fat that has accumulated on top of the liquid.

HELPFUL HINTS

For short-term storage, keep the stock in your refrigerator in a covered container for up to 3 days. For longer storage, divide the stock into 2-cup portions, and pour it into freezer-safe containers; freeze them for up to 3 months. To use frozen stock, thaw it in the refrigerator or in the microwave.

To prepare the stock in a pressure cooker: Combine all ingredients in a 6-quart pressure cooker. Place the lid on the cooker, lock it into position, and place the pressure regulator onto the vent pipe if you're using a first-generation cooker. Over medium-high or high heat, bring the cooker up to pressure. Then, lower the heat, adjusting it as necessary to maintain pressure (regulator should rock gently) and cook the mixture for 35 minutes. Quick-release the pressure (under cold running water if you're using a first-generation cooker). Carefully remove the pressure regulator and lid. Pour the stock through a large strainer into a large bowl or pot. Discard bones, vegetables, and seasonings. Chill the stock, then skim fat that has accumulated on top of the liquid.

No roasted beef ribs on hand? Then pick up some soup bones and roast them in a 375° oven for about an hour. Prepare the stock as per recipe.

PER CUP:
Calories: 47
Fat (g): 1
Saturated Fat (g): 0
Cholesterol (mg): 0
Carbohydrates (g): 7.5
Sodium (mg): 70
Dietary Fiber (g): 0

CHICKEN STOCK

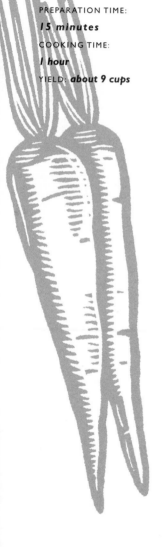

PREPARATION TIME:
15 minutes
COOKING TIME:
1 hour
YIELD: *about 9 cups*

A subtly seasoned, low-sodium stock with just 1 gram of fat.

1	teaspoon olive oil
1	pound chicken breasts
10	cups water
2	celery stalks, leaves included, halved
4	large onions, with skins, quartered
4	medium carrots, halved
1	small turnip, quartered
2	bay leaves
6	cloves garlic
8	whole black peppercorns
10	sage leaves
1	sprig thyme

Warm oil in an 8-quart pot over medium-high heat for 1 minute. Add chicken and cook it until pieces are browned on all sides. Add water, celery, onions, carrots, turnips, bay leaves, garlic, peppercorns, sage, and thyme. Cover pot, and bring stock to a boil. Reduce heat; simmer stock for 1 hour.

Line a colander with cheesecloth. Pour stock through colander into a large bowl or pot. Discard bones, vegetables, and seasonings. Chill stock, then skim fat that has accumulated on top of the liquid.

HELPFUL HINTS

For short-term storage, keep the stock in your refrigerator in a covered container for up to 3 days. For longer storage, divide the stock into 2-cup portions, and pour it into freezer-safe containers; freeze them for up to 3 months. To use frozen stock, thaw it in the refrigerator or in the microwave.

To prepare the stock in a pressure cooker: Warm oil in a large nonstick skillet over medium-high heat for 1 minute. Add chicken and cook it until the pieces are browned on all sides. Transfer the chicken to a 6-quart pressure cooker. Add remaining ingredients. Place the lid on the cooker, lock it into position, and place the pressure regulator onto the vent pipe if you're using a first-generation cooker. Over medium-high or high heat, bring the cooker up to pressure. Then, lower the heat, adjusting it as necessary to maintain pressure (regulator should rock gently) and cook the mixture for 25 minutes. Quick-release the pressure (under cold running water if you're using a first-generation cooker). Carefully remove the pressure regulator and lid. Pour the stock through a large strainer into a large bowl or pot. Discard chicken bones, vegetables, and seasonings; reserve chicken breast meat for another use. Chill the stock, then skim fat that has accumulated on top of the liquid.

PER CUP:
Calories: 40
Fat (g): 1
Saturated Fat (g): 0
Cholesterol (mg): 0
Carbohydrates (g): 6.5
Sodium (mg): 68
Dietary Fiber (g): 0

QUICK SAGE CHICKEN BROTH

Make this light, fresh-tasting broth when you have just 10 minutes to simmer up a flavorful stock. The secret behind the speed? Canned broth.

PREPARATION TIME:
5 minutes
COOKING TIME:
10 minutes
YIELDS: **about 2 cups**

1 can (14 ounces) fat-free chicken broth
1 medium onion, quartered
½ celery stalk
2 sage leaves
2 teaspoons sherry

Combine broth, onion, celery, sage, and sherry in a 2-quart saucepan. Cover pot, and bring broth to a boil. Reduce heat; simmer broth for 10 minutes. Discard vegetables and seasonings.

PER CUP:
Calories: 67
Fat (g): 0.2
Saturated Fat (g): 0
Cholesterol (mg): 0
Carbohydrates (g): 3.5
Sodium (mg): 152
Dietary Fiber (g): 0

VEGETABLE STOCK

This no-salt-added vegetable stock with its light, onion flavor makes a perfect base for many of the soups and stews in this book.

10 cups water
5 onions, with skins, quartered
3 carrots, halved
3 celery stalks with leaves, halved
2 bay leaves
¼ cup packed basil leaves (approximately 10)
10 whole white peppercorns
1 sprig parsley
1 sprig thyme (optional)

PREPARATION TIME:
15 minutes
COOKING TIME:
30 minutes
YIELD: *about 9 cups*

Combine water, onions, carrots, celery, bay leaves, basil, peppercorns, parsley, and thyme, if using, in an 8-quart pot. Cover and bring stock to a boil. Reduce heat and simmer stock for 30 minutes.

Line a colander with cheesecloth. Pour stock through colander into a large bowl or pot. Discard vegetables and seasonings.

HELPFUL HINTS

For short-term storage, keep the stock in your refrigerator in a covered container for up to 3 days. For longer storage, divide the stock into 2-cup portions, and pour it into freezer-safe containers; freeze them for up to 3 months. To use frozen stock, thaw it in the refrigerator or in the microwave.

To prepare the stock in a pressure cooker: Combine all ingredients in a 6-quart pressure cooker. Place the lid on the cooker, lock it into position, and place the pressure regulator onto the vent pipe if you're using a first-generation cooker. Over medium-high or high heat, bring the cooker up to pressure. Then, lower the heat, adjusting it as necessary to maintain pressure (regulator should rock gently) and cook the mixture for 10 minutes. Quick-release the pressure (under cold running water if you're using a first-generation cooker). Carefully remove the pressure regulator and lid. Pour stock through a large strainer into a large bowl or pot. Discard vegetables and seasonings.

PER CUP:
Calories: 50
Fat (g): 0.2
Saturated Fat (g): 0
Cholesterol (mg): 0
Carbohydrates (g): 5.2
Sodium (mg): 31
Dietary Fiber (g): 0

bountiful
bean pot

Black Bean, Rice, and Corn Chili

Black-Eyed Pea and Corn Chowder

Black Magic Garlic Chowder

Butter Beans, Mostaccioli, and Ham

Chili in Black and White

Cincinnati Chili with Attitude

Cranberry Bean Chowder with Zucchini

Ditalini with White Beans and Collards

Fresh Two-Bean Stew with Rosemary

Lentil Chili with Bacon and Beef

Monterey Chili Acini de Pepe

Pigeon Pea Chowder with Spanish Onions

Rice and Adzuki Beans with Vegetables

Sagebrush Chili with Fresh Tomatoes

Scotch Bonnet Chili

Spicy Chili Beans

b o u n t i f u l   b e a n   p o t

BLACK BEAN, RICE, AND CORN CHILI

This vegetarian chili is simple, speedy, and tastes superb. If you'd like more "heat," use a cayenne pepper instead of the jalapeño.

 1 teaspoon olive oil
 1½ cups chopped onions
 3 teaspoons minced garlic
 1 can (28 ounces) crushed tomatoes
 1 can (16 ounces) black beans, rinsed and drained
 ½ cup frozen corn
 ½ cup cooked rice
 1 large red bell pepper, chopped
 1 jalapeño pepper, seeded and minced
 1 tablespoon chili powder
 1 teaspoon allspice

PREPARATION TIME:
10 minutes
COOKING TIME:
25 minutes
SERVINGS: *4*

Warm oil in a 4-quart pot over medium-high heat for 1 minute. Add onions and garlic; sauté mixture until onions are translucent, about 7 minutes.

Stir in tomatoes, beans, corn, rice, bell peppers, jalapeño peppers, chili powder, and allspice. Cover pot, and bring chili to a boil. Reduce heat and simmer for 15 minutes.

HELPFUL HINT

No cooked rice on hand? Then cook up a small batch while you're chopping and sautéing the onions. Simply bring ½ cup water to a boil in a 2- or 3-quart saucepan; stir in ¼ cup long- or medium-grain rice. Cover the pot and cook rice until the water is absorbed and the rice is tender, about 15 minutes.

PER SERVING:
Calories: 258
Fat (g): 2.4
Saturated Fat (g): 0.4
Cholesterol (mg): 0
Carbohydrates (g): 49.1
Sodium (mg): 75
Dietary Fiber (g): 12.8

BLACK-EYED PEA AND CORN CHOWDER

Roasted red peppers and bacon enliven this fuss-free, ready-in-a-flash chowder.

PREPARATION TIME:

5 minutes

COOKING TIME:

20 minutes

SERVINGS: **4**

4 slices turkey bacon
1 cup fat-free chicken broth
1 can (15 ounces) black-eyed peas, rinsed and drained
1 can (14 ounces) cream-style corn
1 cup chopped onions
2 teaspoons minced garlic
1 teaspoon dried savory leaves
¼ teaspoon black pepper
1 cup roasted red peppers

Cook bacon in a 4-quart pot over medium-high heat until it is crisp. Transfer it to a paper-towel-lined plate.

Add broth, peas, corn, onions, garlic, savory, and black pepper. Cover pot, and bring mixture to a boil. Reduce heat, and simmer mixture for 12 minutes.

Stir in roasted peppers; cook chowder until it's hot throughout. Divide chowder among 4 soup bowls. Crumble bacon, and sprinkle it over each serving.

HELPFUL HINT

Using canned roasted red peppers in lieu of roasting fresh ones reduces prep time in this recipe.

PER SERVING:
Calories: 210
Fat (g): 3.8
Saturated Fat (g): 1.2
Cholesterol (mg): 9
Carbohydrates (g): 36.4
Sodium (mg): 268
Dietary Fiber (g): 10.8

BLACK MAGIC GARLIC CHOWDER

Garlic lovers take note: This is a colorful chowder with plenty of palate-appealing garlic flavor, which has been tamed to mild sweetness by light sautéing. The chowder is elegant enough for a dinner party and easy enough for everyday fare.

PREPARATION TIME:
20 minutes
COOKING TIME:
15 minutes
SERVINGS: **4**

1　can (15 ounces) black beans, rinsed and drained
1　can (14 ounces) reduced-sodium vegetable broth
2　teaspoons olive oil
1　garlic head, cloves thinly sliced
2　small serrano peppers, seeded and minced
1　pound plum tomatoes, coarsely chopped
2　cups croutons
½　cup snipped fresh flat-leaf parsley
½　cup nonfat sour cream

Using a hand-held immersion blender, puree ¾ cup beans with ¾ cup broth. Warm oil in a 4-quart pot over medium-high heat for 1 minute. Add garlic and serrano peppers; sauté them until the garlic is golden but not browned.

Stir in the pureed beans, remaining beans, and remaining broth. Cover pot, and cook the chowder until it's hot, 5 to 10 minutes. Stir in tomatoes; heat until hot throughout. Serve topped with croutons, parsley, and a dollop of sour cream.

HELPFUL HINT

Don't let the garlic burn or it will impart a scorched, bitter flavor to the chowder.

PER SERVING:
Calories: 353
Fat (g): 4.2
Saturated Fat (g): 0.7
Cholesterol (mg): 0
Carbohydrates (g): 64.1
Sodium (mg): 234
Dietary Fiber (g): 12.3

BUTTER BEANS, MOSTACCIOLI, AND HAM

This extra-easy recipe has three great things going for it: It's fast to prepare, has a wonderfully subtle anchovy flavor, and is delightfully rich tasting—thanks to Romano cheese.

PREPARATION TIME:

10 minutes

COOKING TIME:

10 minutes

SERVINGS: 4

1 can (15 ounces) small butter beans, rinsed and drained
2 cans (14 ounces each) fat-free chicken broth
4 ounces mostaccioli
¼ pound lean cooked ham, diced
1 can (2 ounces) anchovies, rinsed, drained, and mashed
2 teaspoons garlic
1 small mild chili pepper, chopped
½ cup sliced scallions
¼ cup grated Romano cheese

Combine beans, broth, mostaccioli, ham, anchovies, and garlic in a 4-quart pot. Cover pot, and bring mixture to a boil. Reduce heat, and simmer mixture for 7 minutes.

Add chili peppers, scallions, and Romano cheese; cook chowder for 1 minute.

HELPFUL HINT

For maximum cheese flavor, use freshly grated Romano.

PER SERVING:
Calories: 560
Fat (g): 4.2
Saturated Fat (g): 1.7
Cholesterol (mg): 22
Carbohydrates (g): 91.4
Sodium (mg): 497
Dietary Fiber (g): 21

CHILI IN BLACK AND WHITE

Black beans, white beans, and wild rice give this vegetarian chili a unique, "al dente" texture. Its warm flavor comes from toasted cumin seeds. Toasting, a technique used by Indian cooks, enhances spice flavor.

1   teaspoon olive oil
1   medium onion, chopped
2   cups reduced-sodium tomato juice
2   tablespoons reduced-sodium tomato paste
1   cup cooked black beans, rinsed and drained
1   cup cooked small white beans, rinsed and drained
1   cup cooked wild rice
1   anaheim pepper, seeded and minced
1   teaspoon paprika
1   teaspoon cumin seeds, toasted

Warm oil in a 4-quart pot over medium-high heat for 1 minute. Add onions, and sauté them until they're translucent, about 5 minutes. Stir in tomato juice and tomato paste.

Add black beans, white beans, rice, and anaheim peppers. Cover pot, and simmer chili for 5 minutes. Stir in paprika and cumin; simmer for 1 minute more.

HELPFUL HINTS

For directions on toasting seeds, see "Helpful Hint" under Tenderloin Chili (page 111).

To make 1 cup cooked wild rice: Bring 1 cup water to a boil in a 3-quart saucepan; add $\frac{1}{4}$ cup raw wild rice; cook rice until water has been absorbed and rice is tender, about 50 minutes.

To store leftover tomato paste: Mist a baking sheet with nonstick cooking spray. Arrange tablespoon-size dollops of paste on the baking sheet. Place the sheet in your freezer. When the paste has frozen (it'll take about an hour), wrap each dollop in a small piece of waxed paper and transfer the dollops to a freezer-proof plastic bag. Remove and thaw dollops as needed.

PREPARATION TIME:
10 minutes
COOKING TIME:
15 minutes
SERVINGS: **4**

PER SERVING:
Calories: 435
Fat (g): 2.8
Saturated Fat (g): 0.5
Cholesterol (mg): 0
Carbohydrates (g): 81.1
Sodium (mg): 34
Dietary Fiber (g): 18.1

CINCINNATI CHILI WITH ATTITUDE

Midwesterners have a penchant for chili that's thick and spicy and served over spaghetti. Here, I offer a vegetarian version with lentils, tomatoes, and eight easy-to-find seasonings. I think you'll find this special chili more than meets your expectations.

PREPARATION TIME:

10 minutes

COOKING TIME:

30 minutes

SERVINGS: **6**

1	teaspoon olive oil
1	medium onion, chopped
2	cups cooked lentils
1	can (15 ounces) crushed tomatoes
1	tablespoon minced garlic
2	teaspoons Worcestershire sauce
$1/4$	teaspoon ground allspice
$1/8$	teaspoon ground cloves
1	tablespoon chili powder
1	teaspoon cocoa
$1/4$	teaspoon cinnamon
12	ounces linguine

Warm oil in 4-quart pot over medium-high heat for 1 minute. Add onions, and sauté them until they're translucent, about 5 minutes. Add lentils, tomatoes, garlic, Worcestershire sauce, allspice, cloves, chili powder, cocoa, and cinnamon. Simmer chili for 20 minutes.

Meanwhile, cook linguine according to package directions, omitting salt. Drain linguine. Serve topped with chili.

HELPFUL HINTS

To cook the lentils, bring 2 cups water to a boil in a 3-quart saucepan. Stir in 1 cup lentils; simmer them, covered, until they're tender, 30 to 45 minutes.

To prepare the chili in a slow cooker: Sauté the onions in oil in a skillet over medium-high heat. Transfer them to an electric slow cooker; add the remaining ingredients except the linguine. Cover cooker, and cook the chili on Low for 5 to 7 hours. Cook linguine; serve it topped with the chili.

PER SERVING:
Calories: 327
Fat (g): 2.4
Saturated Fat (g): 0.4
Cholesterol (mg): 0
Carbohydrates (g): 62.8
Sodium (mg): 42
Dietary Fiber (g): 8.4

CRANBERRY BEAN CHOWDER WITH ZUCCHINI

A smidgen of smoked Lebanon bologna adds unique flavor to this heart-warming vegetable-bean stew.

1 teaspoon olive oil
1 medium zucchini, halved lengthwise and sliced
1 can (16 ounces) red cranberry (Roman) beans, rinsed and drained
1 potato, cut into ½-inch cubes
1½ cups fat-free beef broth
1 cup flat green beans, broken into 1-inch lengths
¼ teaspoon freshly ground white pepper
4 scallions, sliced
1 slice (1 ounce) smoked Lebanon bologna, finely chopped

Warm oil in a nonstick skillet over medium-high heat for 1 minute. Add zucchini, and sauté until it is translucent, 8 to 10 minutes. Transfer to a 4-quart pot.

Add red beans, potatoes, broth, green beans, and pepper. Cover pot; bring mixture to a boil. Reduce heat and simmer mixture for 10 minutes. Stir in scallions and bologna; simmer chowder for 2 minutes.

HELPFUL HINT

Whenever possible, use freshly ground black or white pepper. The preground stuff has pepper's bite but little of its flavor.

PREPARATION TIME:
15 minutes
COOKING TIME:
30 minutes
SERVINGS: *4*

PER SERVING:
Calories: 258
Fat (g): 2.7
Saturated Fat (g): 0.7
Cholesterol (mg): 4
Carbohydrates (g): 44.7
Sodium (mg): 145
Dietary Fiber (g): 14.6

DITALINI WITH WHITE BEANS AND COLLARDS

Create a stir with this knockout entrée that's full of beans, pasta, and healthful greens. If you'd like some crunch, top each serving with crispy croutons.

PREPARATION TIME:

15 minutes

COOKING TIME:

20 minutes

SERVINGS: *4*

1 teaspoon olive oil

1 onion, chopped

1 can (16 ounces) diced tomatoes

1 can (14 ounces) reduced-sodium vegetable broth

1 can (15 ounces) small white beans, rinsed and drained

⅔ cup ditalini

1 teaspoon dried oregano

2 cups packed torn collards

2 teaspoons Louisiana-style hot-pepper sauce

2 teaspoons grated lemon peel

2 tablespoons shredded provolone cheese

Warm oil in a 4-quart pot over medium-high heat for 1 minute. Add onions; sauté them until they're soft and translucent.

Add tomatoes, broth, beans, ditalini, and oregano. Cover pot, and bring mixture to a boil. Reduce heat, and simmer mixture until ditalini are al dente, 10 to 12 minutes.

Stir in collards, hot-pepper sauce, lemon peel, and provolone.

HELPFUL HINT

Collards looking kind of shop-worn this week? Then use kale or green cabbage instead.

PER SERVING:
Calories: 315
Fat (g): 3.2
Saturated Fat (g): 0.8
Cholesterol (mg): 2.1
Carbohydrates (g): 58.4
Sodium (mg): 90
Dietary Fiber (g): 15.8

FRESH TWO-BEAN STEW WITH ROSEMARY

Believe it or not, these beans are delightfully crisp-tender—even after simmering, unattended, for hours. And their flavor? It's fresh and pleasantly complemented with rosemary.

PREPARATION TIME:

20 minutes

COOKING TIME:

5 hours (slow cooker)

SERVINGS: **4**

2	slices turkey bacon
1 1/4	cups chopped red onion
1/2	pound Roma green beans
1/2	pound wax beans
1	can (28 ounces) crushed tomatoes with basil
1	medium red potato, cut into 1/2-inch cubes
2	teaspoons minced garlic
1	teaspoon dried rosemary
1/4	teaspoon black pepper

In a nonstick skillet, sauté bacon until it's crisp. Transfer it to a paper-towel-lined plate and set it aside. Add onions to skillet; sauté them until they're translucent. Transfer them to an electric slow cooker.

Add beans, tomatoes, potato, garlic, rosemary, and black pepper. Cover cooker; cook on Low until beans and potatoes are tender, 5 to 7 hours. Stir in bacon.

HELPFUL HINT

When preparing fresh beans, save time by snapping off the ends instead of cutting them.

PER SERVING:
Calories: 190
Fat (g): 1.9
Saturated Fat (g): 0.6
Cholesterol (mg): 4.5
Carbohydrates (g): 36.7
Sodium (mg): 604
Dietary Fiber (g): 8.6

LENTIL CHILI WITH BACON AND BEER

Lime, beer, and bacon make this chili differently delicious. So give it a try; it's a snap to make.

PREPARATION TIME:

15 minutes

COOKING TIME:

25 minutes

SERVINGS: *4*

4 slices lower-sodium bacon

1 medium onion, chopped

1½ cups cooked lentils

1 can (15 ounces) black beans, rinsed and drained

1 cup crushed tomatoes

1 cup beer

1 tablespoon minced garlic

1 tablespoon chili powder

1 jalapeño pepper, seeded and chopped

1 teaspoon ground cumin

1 teaspoon dried rosemary, crushed

Juice of 1 lime

Cook bacon in a large skillet until it is crisp, about 8 minutes. Transfer bacon to a paper-towel-lined plate. Crumble bacon; set it aside. Add onions to skillet; sauté them until they're translucent.

Stir in lentils, beans, tomatoes, beer, garlic, chili powder, jalapeño peppers, cumin, and rosemary. Cover skillet, and simmer mixture for 10 minutes. Stir in lime juice and reserved bacon.

HELPFUL HINT

To cook the lentils, bring 1½ cups water to a boil in a 3-quart saucepan. Stir in ¾ cup lentils; simmer them, covered, until they're tender, 30 to 45 minutes. If you have more lentils than you need for the recipe, freeze the extras for another use.

PER SERVING:
Calories: 304
Fat (g): 3.6
Saturated Fat (g): 1.1
Cholesterol (mg): 5
Carbohydrates (g): 50.2
Sodium (mg): 117
Dietary Fiber (g): 17.4

MONTEREY CHILI ACINI DE PEPE

Some vegetarian chilis call for bulgur, a cracked wheat product that's sometimes difficult to find. This fuss-free and equally satisfying recipe uses acini de pepe, a tiny, readily available pasta instead.

- 1 teaspoon olive oil
- 1 medium onion, chopped
- 1 green bell pepper, chopped
- 1 can (15 ounces) pinto beans, rinsed and drained
- 1 can (14 ounces) diced tomatoes
- 1 tablespoon chili powder
- 1 teaspoon dried oregano
- 1 teaspoon cocoa
- 1/2 cup acini de pepe
- 1/4 cup snipped fresh cilantro
- 1 cup shredded Monterey Jack cheese

PREPARATION TIME:

10 minutes

COOKING TIME:

20 minutes

SERVINGS: *4*

Warm oil in a 4-quart pot over medium-high heat for 1 minute. Add onions and bell peppers; sauté until the onions are translucent, 5 to 7 minutes.

Stir in beans, tomatoes, chili powder, oregano, and cocoa. Cover pot, and bring mixture to a boil. Reduce heat, and simmer mixture for 10 minutes.

Meanwhile, cook acini de pepe according to package directions, omitting salt. Drain and stir pasta into chili mixture. Stir in cilantro. Serve topped with Jack cheese.

HELPFUL HINT

Did you know that cilantro and fresh coriander are one and the same herb? 'Tis true. Both are the leaves of the coriander plant (sometimes called the cilantro plant).

PER SERVING:
Calories: 294
Fat (g): 5.3
Saturated Fat (g): 2.2
Cholesterol (mg): 10
Carbohydrates (g): 47.5
Sodium (mg): 146
Dietary Fiber (g): 12.5

PIGEON PEA CHOWDER WITH SPANISH ONIONS

Ready for a hearty farmer's chowder? This one reflects the Spanish colonial culinary tradition that makes Cuban and Puerto Rican cooking delightfully distinctive.

PREPARATION TIME:

20 minutes

COOKING TIME:

25 minutes

SERVINGS: **4**

2   teaspoons peanut oil
1   large Spanish onion, coarsely chopped
4   shallots, thinly sliced
2   cups shredded zucchini
6   tomatillos, diced
1   large potato, cubed
1   can (15 ounces) green pigeon peas, rinsed and drained
1   cup reduced-sodium vegetable broth
¼   cup sofrito sauce

Warm oil in a 4-quart pot over medium-high heat for 1 minute. Add onions and shallots; sauté until they're translucent.

Add zucchini, tomatillos, potatoes, and peas. Stir in broth. Cover pot, and bring chowder to a boil. Reduce heat, and simmer chowder until potatoes are tender, about 15 minutes. Stir in sofrito.

HELPFUL HINT

Wondering where in the world you'll find pigeon peas? Ponder no more. They're available in the canned bean section of most large supermarkets.

PER SERVING:
Calories: 354
Fat (g): 6.6
Saturated Fat (g): 1.7
Cholesterol (mg): 5
Carbohydrates (g): 63.8
Sodium (mg): 175
Dietary Fiber (g): 11.5

RICE AND ADZUKI BEANS WITH VEGETABLES

In this easy khichuri, a classic Indian grain-and-bean stew, adzuki beans, which are slightly sweet, replace the usual dal, or legume. Inspiration for this spicy concoction came from Bharti Kirchner's cookbook, "Indian Inspired."

PREPARATION TIME:

15 minutes

COOKING TIME:

25 minutes

SERVINGS: **4**

1 can (15 ounces) adzuki beans, rinsed and drained
½ cup long-grain rice
2 cans chicken broth
¼ teaspoon turmeric
1 teaspoon ground cumin
1 teaspoon minced gingerroot
1 small jalapeño pepper, seeded and minced
3 carrots, thinly sliced
2 cups cut wax beans
4 plum tomatoes, coarsely chopped
¼ cup toasted sunflower seeds

Combine beans, rice, broth, turmeric, cumin, gingerroot, jalapeño peppers, carrots, and wax beans in a 4-quart pot. Cover pot, and bring mixture to a boil. Reduce heat, and simmer mixture until vegetables and rice are tender, 16 to 20 minutes.

Stir in tomatoes; cook 2 minutes more. Top each serving with sunflower seeds.

HELPFUL HINT

For directions on toasting seeds, see "Helpful Hint" under Tenderloin Chili (page 111).

PER SERVING:
Calories: 324
Fat (g): 5.2
Saturated Fat (g): 0.6
Cholesterol (mg): 0
Carbohydrates (g): 50.9
Sodium (mg): 189
Dietary Fiber (g): 6.1

SAGEBRUSH CHILI WITH FRESH TOMATOES

For a fresh take on an old Southwestern favorite, this high-flavor chili sports ripe tomatoes and silver-green sage leaves.

PREPARATION TIME:

15 minutes

COOKING TIME:

15 minutes

SERVINGS: *4*

2 teaspoons olive oil

4 scallions, sliced

8 cloves garlic, thinly sliced

4 cups tomato wedges

2 cups canned pinto beans, rinsed and drained

1 large yellow cayenne pepper, roasted, seeded, and minced

2 tablespoons chili powder

1 teaspoon ground cumin

$\frac{1}{2}$ teaspoon coriander

6 fresh sage leaves, snipped

Warm oil in a 3-quart saucepan over medium-high heat for 1 minute. Add scallions and garlic; sauté for 3 minutes.

Add tomatoes, beans, cayenne peppers, chili powder, cumin, and coriander. Cover pan; heat chili until tomatoes soften, about 4 minutes. Stir in sage; cook chili, uncovered, for 1 minute more.

HELPFUL HINT

For ease and speed, I roast whole peppers on a hot grill, then seed and mince them.

PER SERVING:

Calories: 191

Fat (g): 4

Saturated Fat (g): 0.6

Cholesterol (mg): 0

Carbohydrates (g): 32.9

Sodium (mg): 55

Dietary Fiber (g): 10.6

SCOTCH BONNET CHILI

A true "hot-heads" delight, this chili gets its firepower from the redoubtable habanero pepper. Often called Scotch bonnet, the habanero and bonnet chilies are actually close relatives, with a similar characteristic shape and bright orange color.

PREPARATION TIME:
15 minutes
COOKING TIME:
25 minutes
SERVINGS: **4**

1 teaspoon olive oil

1 large onion, chopped

¼ pound cooked smoked sausage, halved lengthwise and sliced

1 medium green bell pepper, chopped

1 habanero pepper, chopped

2 cups canned whole tomatoes, cut up

2 cups fat-free refried beans

1 tablespoon chili powder

1 teaspoon ground cumin

1 cup fat-free sour cream

Warm oil in a 4-quart pot over medium-high heat for 1 minute. Add onions, sausage, bell peppers, and habanero peppers; sauté until the onions are translucent, about 5 minutes.

Stir in tomatoes, beans, chili powder, and cumin; simmer, uncovered, until mixture is heated through and thickened slightly, about 15 minutes. Top each serving with sour cream.

HELPFUL HINTS

Chopping and refrigerating habanero peppers a day before using them will lessen the fire but keep the wonderful, almost smoky flavor.

To cook this chili in a slow cooker: Sauté the onions, sausage, bell peppers, and habanero peppers in a large skillet until the onions are translucent. Transfer the mixture to an electric slow cooker. Stir in the remaining ingredients except the sour cream. Cover the cooker and cook the chili on Low for 5 to 7 hours. Serve with the sour cream.

PER SERVING:
Calories: 274
Fat (g): 8.2
Saturated Fat (g): 1.1
Cholesterol (mg): 25
Carbohydrates (g): 38.5
Sodium (mg): 332
Dietary Fiber (g): 5.5

SPICY CHILI BEANS

On a cold winter's night, nothing chases chills better than this easy-to-prepare vegetarian dish, and it's ready to serve in just 20 minutes.

PREPARATION TIME:
10 minutes
COOKING TIME:
20 minutes
SERVINGS: *4*

1 can (14 ounces) chili beans
1 cup fat-free beef broth
1 can (14 ounces) plum tomatoes, juice reserved for another use
   and tomatoes cut up
2 green bell peppers, chopped
1 cup frozen corn
1 onion, chopped
2 teaspoons minced garlic
1 teaspoon chili powder

Combine beans, broth, tomatoes, peppers, corn, onions, garlic, and chili powder in a 4-quart pot.

Cover pot, and bring chili to a boil. Reduce heat, and simmer the chili for 15 to 20 minutes to blend flavors.

HELPFUL HINT

To make this chili in a slow cooker: Simply put everything into the cooker. Cover it and cook the chili on Low for 5 to 6 hours or on High for 3 to 4 hours.

PER SERVING:
Calories: 196
Fat (g): 1.5
Saturated Fat (g): 0.5
Cholesterol (mg): 0
Carbohydrates (g): 43.5
Sodium (mg): 345
Dietary Fiber (g): 10.5

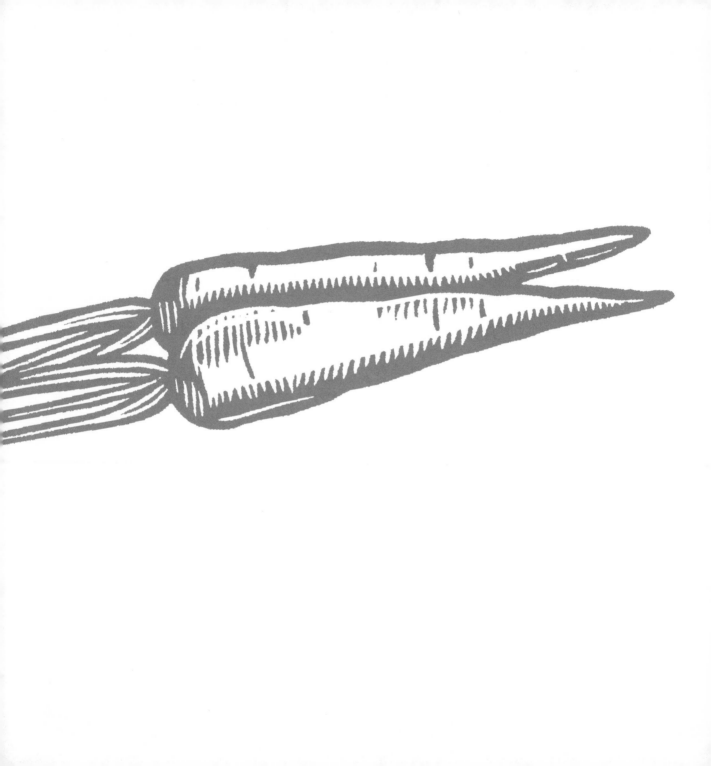

vegetable patch perfection

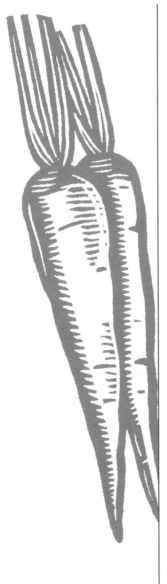

Acorn Squash Stew with Kielbasa

Cheese Ravioli with Basil

Chervil-Seasoned Tortellini

Chili-Stuffed Peppers

Florida Avocado and Tomato Chowder

French Vegetable Chowder with Pistou

Fresh Tomato-Zucchini Chowder

Leek Chowder with Ham

Shiitake-Portobello Chowder

Ragout of Winter Vegetables

Ratatouille with Zucchini and Feta

Thai-Spiced Carrots and Chicken

Vegetarian Chili with Sharp Cheddar

Vegetarian Chili 'Wiches

v e g e t a b l e   p a t c h   p e r f e c t i o n

ACORN SQUASH STEW WITH KIELBASA

I love the way just a little kielbasa, a smoked Polish sausage, perks up this chunky, vegetable-rich stew.

1 teaspoon olive oil
¼ pound turkey kielbasa, halved lengthwise and thinly sliced
1 can (14 ounces) fat-free beef broth
2 pounds acorn squash, peeled, seeded, and cut into 1-inch cubes
1 medium onion, cut into thin wedges
1 can (15 ounces) stewed tomatoes
1½ cups frozen peas
2 tablespoons instant flour

Warm oil in a 4-quart pot over medium-high heat for 1 minute. Add sausage and sauté until it's lightly browned, about 3 minutes.

Stir in broth, squash, onions, and tomatoes. Cover pot; simmer mixture for 10 minutes. Stir in peas; simmer stew until it's hot throughout and vegetables are tender, about 3 minutes. Slowly stir in flour; cook stew until it has thickened, about 3 minutes.

HELPFUL HINT

No question about it: Peeling and cutting hard-shelled winter squash, such as acorn, butternut, and Hubbard, takes some oomph. To make the task easier, use a sturdy, sharp chef's knife. And do the peeling before scraping out the seeds and cubing the flesh.

PREPARATION TIME:
20 minutes
COOKING TIME:
25 minutes
SERVINGS: **4**

PER SERVING:
Calories: 233
Fat (g): 3.8
Saturated Fat (g): 1
Cholesterol (mg): 18
Carbohydrates (g): 39.8
Sodium (mg): 603
Dietary Fiber (g): 5

CHEESE RAVIOLI WITH BASIL

Love ravioli? In the mood for a stew? This dish promises both, and it's packed with fresh vegetables—squash, tomatoes, carrots, and escarole—to boot.

PREPARATION TIME:

15 minutes

COOKING TIME:

25 minutes

SERVINGS: *4*

  2 cans reduced-sodium vegetable broth
  2 carrots, cut into thin 2-inch-long strips
1 1/4 cups chopped yellow squash
  3 plum tomatoes, coarsely chopped
  1 package (about 20 ounces) frozen small round cheese ravioli
  1/2 teaspoon crushed red pepper flakes
  2 cups torn fresh escarole
  1/2 cup snipped fresh basil

Combine the broth and carrots in a 4-quart pot. Cover pot, and bring mixture to a boil. Reduce heat, and simmer mixture until carrots are tender, about 10 minutes. Add squash, tomatoes, and ravioli; cook stew until squash is tender and ravioli is hot throughout, 8 to 12 minutes.

Stir in red pepper, escarole, and basil. Cook stew for 1 minute.

HELPFUL HINT

Take care not to overcook the stew or the ravioli will become soggy.

PER SERVING:
Calories: 467
Fat (g): 8.7
Saturated Fat (g): 3.3
Cholesterol (mg): 97
Carbohydrates (g): 74.2
Sodium (mg): 644
Dietary Fiber (g): 6.6

CHERVIL-SEASONED TORTELLINI

Got a few minutes? All you'll need is about 15 to throw together this extra-easy, extra-tasty dish of cheese-stuffed tortellini. To turn it into a vegetarian entrée, simply replace the chicken broth with a vegetable variety.

PREPARATION TIME:

15 minutes

COOKING TIME:

10 minutes

SERVINGS: *4*

 1 can (15 ounces) stewed tomatoes
 2 cans (14 ounces each) fat-free chicken broth
 $\frac{1}{2}$ teaspoon allspice
 2 cups (1 pound) frozen tri-color cheese tortellini
 1 green bell pepper, chopped
 $\frac{1}{2}$ teaspoon dried chervil
 1 tablespoon snipped fresh basil, *or* $\frac{1}{2}$ teaspoon dried

Combine tomatoes, broth, and allspice in a 4-quart pot. Cover pot and bring mixture to a boil; stir in tortellini, peppers, and chervil. Reduce heat; simmer stew until tortellini are hot, about 10 minutes. Stir in basil.

HELPFUL HINT

If you purchase fresh tortellini, follow the instructions for cooking time.

PER SERVING:
Calories: 197
Fat (g): 3.1
Saturated Fat (g): 1.3
Cholesterol (mg): 10
Carbohydrates (g): 29.6
Sodium (mg): 568
Dietary Fiber (g): 3.3

CHILI-STUFFED PEPPERS

Always popular, always colorful, stuffed peppers make for a dynamite dish, especially when filled with a chili that's seasoned to appeal to the senses, as this one does.

PREPARATION TIME:

20 minutes

COOKING TIME:

20 minutes

SERVINGS: **4**

1⅓ cups vegetable protein crumbles
1 medium onion, chopped
1 can (15 ounces) crushed tomatoes
2 teaspoons minced garlic
1 yellow cayenne pepper, seeded and minced
1 tablespoon chili powder
1 teaspoon ground cumin
4 large orange, *or* yellow, bell peppers, halved, seeded, and blanched
4 ounces reduced-sodium Cheddar cheese, cut into 4 slices

Combine vegetable crumbles, onions, tomatoes, garlic, cayenne peppers, chili powder, and cumin in a 3-quart saucepan. Cook over medium heat until flavors are blended, about 15 minutes.

Arrange bell pepper halves in a broiler-safe pan; divide chili among the halves. Top each with half a Cheddar slice. Broil peppers until Cheddar melts, 2 to 3 minutes.

HELPFUL HINT

Here are two easy ways to blanch pepper halves:

Bring a 4-quart pot of water to boiling. Drop in the peppers. Cook them for 2 minutes. Immediately drain and cool them under *cold* running water.*

Or place peppers in a microwave-safe bowl. Fill the bowl halfway with water and cover it with vented plastic. Microwave the peppers on High for 3 minutes. Immediately drain and cool them under cold running water.*

*Note: Cook the peppers in two or three batches if the pot or bowl is crowded.

PER SERVING:
Calories: 272
Fat (g): 8.3
Saturated Fat (g): 3.1
Cholesterol (mg): 20
Carbohydrates (g): 38.7
Sodium (mg): 660
Dietary Fiber (g): 7.4

FLORIDA AVOCADO AND TOMATO CHOWDER

In this easy recipe, corn, tomatoes, avocado, and smoked turkey create a kaleidoscope of fresh color and flavors. Bacon, lime, and thyme complete the sensory experience.

2 slices bacon
3 large potatoes, peeled and cut into ½-inch cubes
1 can (14 ounces) fat-free chicken broth
1 teaspoon ground thyme
½ pound deli smoked turkey breast, cut into ½-inch cubes
1 cup frozen corn
4 plum tomatoes, coarsely chopped
1 Florida avocado, peeled and cut into ½-inch cubes
Juice of 1 lime
½ teaspoon freshly ground black pepper

PREPARATION TIME:
20 minutes
COOKING TIME:
25 minutes
SERVINGS: **4**

Cook bacon in a 4-quart pot until it is crisp. Transfer bacon to a paper-towel-lined plate. Crumble bacon. Wipe fat from pot.

Combine potatoes, broth, and thyme in same pot. Cover pot, and bring mixture to a boil. Reduce heat, and simmer mixture until potatoes are tender, about 15 minutes. Using a slotted spoon, transfer half of potatoes to a bowl; keep them warm.

Using an immersion blender, puree potatoes in pot. Add turkey, corn, and reserved potatoes; simmer for 3 to 5 minutes. Stir in tomatoes, avocado, juice, black pepper, and reserved bacon. Serve chowder immediately.

HELPFUL HINT

When exposed to air, avocados oxidize, or turn brown, quickly, so cut them right before serving.

PER SERVING:
Calories: 364
Fat (g): 9.4
Saturated Fat (g): 2.1
Cholesterol (mg): 50
Carbohydrates (g): 47.4
Sodium (mg): 173
Dietary Fiber (g): 8.8

FRENCH VEGETABLE CHOWDER WITH PISTOU

A complete meal in itself, this chowder has a lively French twist: pistou. Pistou is the French version of Italy's pesto. Bon Appétit!

PREPARATION TIME:
20 minutes
COOKING TIME:
30 minutes
SERVINGS: 4

1 cup rinsed and drained white beans
1 can reduced-sodium vegetable broth
1 large potato, cut into $\frac{1}{2}$-inch cubes
2 carrots, thinly sliced
1 cup cut wax beans
1 cup small cauliflower florets
2 zucchini, cut into $\frac{1}{2}$-inch cubes
1 cup cooked elbow macaroni
3 plum tomatoes, coarsely chopped
4 scallions
$\frac{1}{3}$ cup pistou (see Helpful Hint below)

In a food processor, puree white beans in 1 cup broth. Set aside. Combine potato, carrots, wax beans, and remaining broth in a 4-quart pot; simmer mixture for 15 minutes. Stir in cauliflower and zucchini; simmer mixture for 10 minutes.

Stir in macaroni, tomatoes, scallions, and pureed beans; warm chowder until hot throughout. Stir in pistou and serve chowder immediately.

HELPFUL HINT

To make pistou—a blend of basil, garlic, and cheese—combine 1 tablespoon minced garlic, 2 teaspoons olive oil, $\frac{1}{2}$ cup snipped fresh basil, and $\frac{1}{4}$ cup crumbled blue cheese in a bowl. Mash the mixture with a fork.

PER SERVING:
Calories: 300
Fat (g): 7.5
Saturated Fat (g): 3.2
Cholesterol (mg): 11
Carbohydrates (g): 47.9
Sodium (mg): 272
Dietary Fiber (g): 10.8

FRESH TOMATO-ZUCCHINI CHOWDER

Savor summer's bounty in this lively chowder of basil, tomatoes, and zucchini. Bacon adds a delightful—and I might add, irreplaceable—salty richness.

2 slices turkey bacon

1 cup chopped onion

1 can (14 ounces) vegetable broth

1 medium potato, cut into 3/4-inch cubes

1 cup diced zucchini

1 1/4 cups frozen corn

1 pound plum tomatoes, sliced

1/4 teaspoon ground cayenne pepper

1/4 cup snipped fresh basil

Cook bacon in a 4-quart pot until it is crisp. Transfer bacon to a paper-towel-lined plate. Crumble bacon and set it aside. Add onions to pot; cook until they're translucent.

Add broth, potato, zucchini, corn, tomatoes, and cayenne. Cover pot, and bring chowder to a boil. Reduce heat, and simmer chowder until potatoes are tender, 15 to 20 minutes. Stir in fresh basil. Top each serving with crumbled bacon.

HELPFUL HINT

For the fastest, easiest way to snip basil, stack the leaves one on top of the other. Roll up the leaves lengthwise, then snip across the roll.

PREPARATION TIME:

10 minutes

COOKING TIME:

30 minutes

SERVINGS: *4*

PER SERVING:
Calories: 182
Fat (g): 2.4
Saturated Fat (g): 0.6
Cholesterol (mg): 4.5
Carbohydrates (g): 38.1
Sodium (mg): 158
Dietary Fiber (g): 5.5

LEEK CHOWDER WITH HAM

This chowder is thick and creamy and brimming with leeks and ham, not delicate and light as many leek soups are. Horseradish mustard and Worcestershire sauce team up to give the dish a flavor that's especially pleasing and memorable.

PREPARATION TIME:

15 minutes

COOKING TIME:

30 minutes

SERVINGS: *4*

1 teaspoon olive oil
$\frac{1}{2}$ pound cooked lean ham, cut into $\frac{1}{2}$-inch cubes
3 leeks, white part only, sliced
1 can (14 ounces) fat-free chicken broth
2 large Idaho potatoes (about 1 pound), peeled and cut into $\frac{1}{4}$-inch cubes
1 bay leaf
1 teaspoon horseradish mustard
1 teaspoon Worcestershire sauce
$\frac{1}{2}$ cup skim milk

Warm oil in a 4-quart pot over medium-high heat for 1 minute. Add ham and leeks; cook until leeks are translucent (do not brown), 6 to 8 minutes. Transfer ham and leeks to a bowl; keep them warm.

Combine broth, potatoes, and bay leaf in the same pot. Cover pot, and bring mixture to a boil. Reduce heat, and simmer mixture until potatoes are tender, about 15 minutes. Discard bay leaf. Using a hand-held immersion blender, puree potatoes.

Stir in mustard, Worcestershire sauce, milk, and reserved ham and leeks. Heat chowder until it's hot throughout.

PER SERVING:
Calories: 222
Fat (g): 3.8
Saturated Fat (g): 1.1
Cholesterol (mg): 28
Carbohydrates (g): 32.4
Sodium (mg): 580
Dietary Fiber (g): 2.8

HELPFUL HINT

Leeks can be a sandy lot. To clean them, slit each one lengthwise, then swish it in a sinkful of cold water. Rinse each under cool running water.

SHIITAKE-PORTOBELLO CHOWDER

Celebrate a rich marriage of distinctive mushrooms! The party also features a heavenly broth that weds proper Gruyère cheese with sensuous marsala wine.

2   teaspoons butter
4   shallots (about 8 ounces), thinly sliced
2   large (about 1 pound) potatoes, cut into ¼-inch cubes
3   cups fat-free beef broth
4   ounces shiitake mushroom caps
2   cups cubed portobello mushrooms
¼   cup shredded Gruyère cheese
⅛   teaspoon white pepper
2   tablespoons marsala wine

PREPARATION TIME:
15 minutes
COOKING TIME:
30 minutes
SERVINGS: 4

Melt 1 teaspoon butter in a 4-quart pot. Add shallots; cook them until they're translucent, about 3 minutes, stirring often. Add potatoes and broth; simmer mixture until potatoes are tender, about 15 minutes.

Meanwhile, melt remaining butter in a nonstick skillet. Add shiitake and portobello mushrooms; sauté them until they're wilted and golden brown, about 8 minutes.

When potatoes are tender, puree them using a hand-held immersion blender. Stir mushrooms into the potato puree. Stir in Gruyère, pepper, and wine. Heat chowder until it's hot throughout and Gruyère has melted. Serve it immediately.

HELPFUL HINT

When cleaning mushrooms, wipe them with a damp paper towel or briefly rinse them under cool running water, but never soak them. They'll absorb too much water, which will dilute their subtle flavor.

PER SERVING:
Calories: 593
Fat (g): 5.2
Saturated Fat (g): 2.8
Cholesterol (mg): 13
Carbohydrates (g): 120.7
Sodium (mg): 202
Dietary Fiber (g): 10.5

RAGOUT OF WINTER VEGETABLES

On a chilly day, there's something soul-warming about a stew, like this one, that's brimming with mushrooms, onions, and sturdy vegetables, such as sweet potatoes and carrots. Thyme, garlic, and black pepper provide just-right seasonings.

PREPARATION TIME:

20 minutes

COOKING TIME:

1 hour

SERVINGS: *4*

2   teaspoons olive oil
8   ounces mushrooms, quartered
1   large onion, chopped
3   cloves garlic, minced
2   cans (14 ounces each) fat-free beef broth
1/2 cup mixed wild rice and long-grain rice
3   small sweet potatoes, cut into 3/4-inch cubes
2   carrots, cut into 1/2-inch slices
1   teaspoon thyme
1/4 teaspoon freshly ground black pepper

Warm oil in a 4-quart pot over medium-high heat for 1 minute. Add mushrooms, onions, and garlic; sauté until mushrooms are lightly browned and onions, translucent. Stir in broth. Cover pot, and bring mixture to a boil. Reduce heat, stir in rice, and simmer mixture for 35 minutes.

Stir in potatoes, carrots, thyme, and pepper. Cover pot, and simmer stew until rice, potatoes, and carrots are tender, 15 to 20 minutes.

HELPFUL HINT

If you buy loose carrot bunches with the greens still attached, be sure the greens are crisp, not wilted. To store loose carrots, cut off and discard the tops and stash the carrots in a plastic bag in your fridge.

PER SERVING:
Calories: 269
Fat (g): 5.7
Saturated Fat (g): 0.9
Cholesterol (mg): 0
Carbohydrates (g): 48.6
Sodium (mg): 218
Dietary Fiber (g): 5.6

RATATOUILLE WITH ZUCCHINI AND FETA

Feta, a Greek cheese, imparts a welcome zing to this Mediterranean gem that's brimming with eggplant, tomatoes, and zucchini. For crunch, serve ratatouille with plain or garlic croutons.

2   teaspoons olive oil

2   medium onions, sliced into thin wedges

1   medium (12 ounces) eggplant, peeled and cut into ¾-inch cubes

1   can (28 ounces) whole tomatoes, cut up

2   small zucchini, halved lengthwise and thinly sliced

1   yellow bell pepper, thinly sliced

3   teaspoons minced garlic

2   teaspoons Italian herb seasoning

¼   teaspoon freshly ground black pepper

3   ounces feta cheese, crumbled

Warm oil in a 4-quart pot over medium-high heat for 1 minute. Add onions, and sauté for 1 minute. Add eggplant, and sauté vegetables for 5 minutes.

Stir in tomatoes, zucchini, bell peppers, garlic, and herb seasoning. Cover pot, and bring stew to a boil. Reduce heat, and simmer stew for 20 minutes. Stir in black pepper. Serve each portion topped with feta.

HELPFUL HINT

The easiest way to cut up whole canned tomatoes is to dump them into a 4-cup measure or a 2-quart mixing bowl. Then, using kitchen scissors, snip the tomatoes into smaller pieces.

PREPARATION TIME:
15 minutes
COOKING TIME:
30 minutes
SERVINGS: *4*

PER SERVING:
Calories: 188
Fat (g): 7.9
Saturated Fat (g): 3.7
Cholesterol (mg): 19
Carbohydrates (g): 26
Sodium (mg): 263
Dietary Fiber (g): 6.2

THAI-SPICED CARROTS AND CHICKEN

Peanut sauce, gingerroot, and sesame oil put plenty of Asian-style pizzazz into this dish. And it's a pleasure to make.

PREPARATION TIME:
15 minutes

COOKING TIME:
20 minutes

SERVINGS: **4**

1 pound boneless, skinless chicken breast, cut into $\frac{1}{2}$-inch cubes
4 carrots, cut into thin strips
1 tablespoon minced gingerroot
1 teaspoon minced garlic
1 can (14 ounces) fat-free chicken broth
1 tablespoon reduced-sodium soy sauce
1 cup long-grain rice
$\frac{3}{4}$ cup sliced scallions
1 tablespoon Thai peanut sauce (satay sauce)
1 teaspoon sugar
$\frac{1}{2}$ teaspoon sesame oil

Combine chicken, carrots, gingerroot, garlic, broth, and soy sauce in a 4-quart pot. Cover pot; simmer mixture until chicken is cooked through and carrots are tender, about 15 minutes.

Meanwhile, cook rice according to package directions.

Stir scallions, peanut sauce, sugar, and oil into chicken mixture. Cook stew 5 minutes more. Serve it over hot rice.

HELPFUL HINTS

Don't peek at cooking rice. Here's why: When you lift the pot lid, condensation drips onto the rice. The result is gummy rice.

Here's an emergency substitute if you can't find Thai peanut sauce: Use 1 tablespoon peanut butter (either creamy or chunky) and $\frac{1}{2}$ teaspoon crushed red pepper flakes.

PER SERVING:
Calories: 436
Fat (g): 6
Saturated Fat (g): 1.5
Cholesterol (mg): 96
Carbohydrates (g): 49.6
Sodium (mg): 410
Dietary Fiber (g): 3.5

VEGETARIAN CHILI WITH SHARP CHEDDAR

For a super supper, try this rustic-style dish in which salsa, chilies, and Cheddar cheese jazz up earthy barley, beans, and corn.

PREPARATION TIME:
5 minutes
COOKING TIME:
15 minutes
SERVINGS: 4

1 cup canned red kidney beans, rinsed and drained
1 ½ cups frozen corn
1 ½ cups cooked barley
1 ½ cups canned crushed tomatoes
½ cup medium salsa
2 teaspoons chili powder
1 teaspoon cocoa
1 mild chili pepper, minced
½ cup shredded extra-sharp Cheddar cheese

Combine beans, corn, barley, tomatoes, salsa, chili powder, cocoa, and chili peppers in a 3-quart saucepan. Cover pot; simmer mixture for 10 minutes. Top each serving with Cheddar.

HELPFUL HINT

To make 1 ½ cups of cooked barley, bring 1 ½ cups water to boiling in a 3-quart saucepan. Stir in ½ cup barley. Cover pan and simmer the barley gently until it's tender and the water has been absorbed, about 50 minutes.

PER SERVING:
Calories: 251
Fat (g): 2.5
Saturated Fat (g): 0.8
Cholesterol (mg): 5
Carbohydrates (g): 46.8
Sodium (mg): 510
Dietary Fiber (g): 9.5

VEGETARIAN CHILI 'WICHES

Wow the young and young-at-heart with these speedy, sloppy-Joe sandwiches. They're easy. They're spicy. They're a big hit!

PREPARATION TIME:
5 minutes
COOKING TIME:
15 minutes
SERVINGS: **4**

1 1/3 cups vegetable protein crumbles
1 can (15 ounces) crushed tomatoes
1 small yellow squash, diced
1/2 yellow bell pepper, diced
1/2 of 1 1/2-ounce package prepared chili seasoning
1 jalapeño pepper, seeded and minced
4 Kaiser rolls, split

Combine crumbles, tomatoes, squash, bell peppers, chili seasoning, and jalapeño peppers in a 3-quart saucepan. Cook, covered, until the chili is hot and flavors have blended, about 15 minutes, stirring occasionally. Spoon into the split rolls.

HELPFUL HINT

Here's a quick way to core bell peppers: Cut pepper in half, without cutting through the stem. Starting at the end opposite the stem, carefully pull the pepper apart. The core will automatically separate at the shoulders.

To make this chili in a slow cooker: Combine all ingredients except rolls in an electric slow cooker. Cover cooker and cook chili on Low for 5 to 7 hours or on High for 3 to 4 hours.

PER SERVING:
Calories: 294
Fat (g): 5.9
Saturated Fat (g): 0.5
Cholesterol (mg): 0
Carbohydrates (g): 53.6
Sodium (mg): 589
Dietary Fiber (g): 6.7

sensational

seafood

sampler

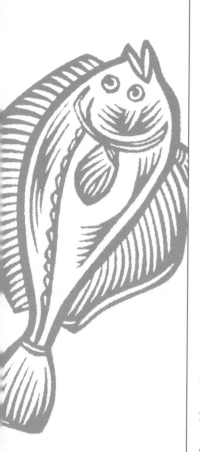

Caribbean-Style Flounder

Crab Chowder with Snow Peas

Creamy Clam and Broccoli Chowder

Curried Scallops and Potato Chowder

Easy Manhattan Clam Chowder

Halibut and Potato Chowder

Lighthouse Clam Chowder

Lobster and Shrimp Chowder

Mediterranean Fishermen's Stew

Monkfish-Cheddar Chowder

Salmon and Roasted Pepper Chowder

Seafood Sampler

Shrimp and Baby Vegetables

Shrimp and Sausage Gumbo

Spicy Crab and Scallop Chowder

Thai-Style Shrimp and Sweet Peppers

CARIBBEAN-STYLE FLOUNDER

Here's my version of an ideal island-fisherman's feast: A fuss-free, flavorful dish of flounder, sweet potatoes, and tomatoes that's done to perfection in less than 30 minutes.

2 teaspoons peanut oil

1 tablespoon annatto seeds

1 medium onion, thinly sliced

2 cups fat-free chicken broth

1 sweet potato (about ½ pound), cut into ½-inch cubes

1 can (14 ounces) whole tomatoes, cut up

1 teaspoon thyme

1 cup frozen peas

1 pound flounder filet, cut into ¾-inch cubes

4 teaspoons lemon juice

Warm oil in a 4-quart pot over medium-high heat for 1 minute. Add annatto seeds and sauté for 3 minutes. Using a slotted spoon, remove seeds and discard them. Add onions to pot; sauté for 2 minutes.

Add broth, potatoes, tomatoes, and thyme. Cover pot, and bring mixture to a boil. Reduce heat, and simmer mixture until potatoes are tender, about 10 minutes. Using a potato masher or back of a fork, mash potatoes.

Add peas and flounder; simmer soup for 10 minutes more. Stir in lemon juice.

HELPFUL HINT

Flounder is a delicate fish. So stir the chowder gently; otherwise, the flounder will fall apart.

PREPARATION TIME:

10 minutes

COOKING TIME:

30 minutes

SERVINGS: *4*

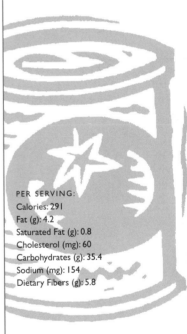

PER SERVING:
Calories: 291
Fat (g): 4.2
Saturated Fat (g): 0.8
Cholesterol (mg): 60
Carbohydrates (g): 35.4
Sodium (mg): 154
Dietary Fibers (g): 5.8

CRAB CHOWDER WITH SNOW PEAS

This classy chowder gets its sensual, perfumy essence from jasmine rice, gingerroot, and sorrel. The crab meat is canned, eliminating the need to pick meat from shells.

PREPARATION TIME:

10 minutes

COOKING TIME:

25 minutes

SERVINGS: *4*

PER SERVING:

Calories: 242
Fat (g): 5.3
Saturated Fat (g): 2.4
Cholesterol (mg): 68
Carbohydrates (g): 28.5
Sodium (mg): 648
Dietary Fiber (g): 3.1

2	cups clam juice
2½	cups water
½	cup jasmine rice
2	scallions
1	tablespoon minced gingerroot
2	cans (4 ounces each) lump crab meat
2	cups snow peas, halved crosswise
1	tablespoon sherry
½	cup half-and-half cream
2	cups torn sorrel leaves

Combine clam juice and water in a 4-quart pot; bring mixture to a boil. Stir in rice, scallions, and gingerroot; reduce heat and cook mixture for 20 minutes.

Stir in crab meat and snow peas; simmer for 1 minute. Stir in sherry, half-and-half, and sorrel.

HELPFUL HINT

If jasmine rice isn't available, use basmati or wild pecan rice instead. Just be sure to check the package directions and adjust the cooking time if necessary.

CREAMY CLAM AND BROCCOLI CHOWDER

An unforgettable chowder with a smooth, pureed white-bean base. Cooking time is less than 10 minutes.

2 cups navy beans, *or other small white beans*
1 can (14 ounces) fat-free chicken broth
1 teaspoon olive oil
4 teaspoons minced garlic
1½ cups small broccoli florets
2 cans (6½ ounces each) minced clams, rinsed and drained
4 plum tomatoes, coarsely chopped
2 tablespoons dry white wine
2 tablespoons half-and-half cream
2 tablespoons snipped fresh dill

In a food processor or using a hand-held immersion blender, puree half the beans in ½ cup broth. Set mixture aside. Warm oil in a 4-quart pot over medium-high heat for 1 minute. Add garlic and sauté it for 1 minute.

Add broccoli, remaining broth, and remaining beans; simmer broccoli until it's tender, about 4 minutes. Stir in clams. Heat mixture for 1 minute. Stir in tomatoes, wine, cream, and dill. Warm, then serve immediately.

HELPFUL HINT

After stirring in the tomatoes and wine, keep cooking to a minimum so the cream doesn't curdle.

PREPARATION TIME:

10 minutes

COOKING TIME:

10 minutes

SERVINGS: 4

PER SERVING:
Calories: 358
Fat (g): 7.1
Saturated Fat (g): 1.4
Cholesterol (mg): 64
Carbohydrates (g): 36.3
Sodium (mg): 171
Dietary Fiber (g): 11.6

CURRIED SCALLOPS AND POTATO CHOWDER

Create a stir with this sensational soup. It's got a lively curry flavor and bright yellow color and takes just 20 to 25 minutes to cook.

PREPARATION TIME:
5 minutes
COOKING TIME:
25 minutes
SERVINGS: **4**

1 can (11 ounces) clam juice
1/2 cup dry white wine
2 potatoes (about 1 pound), peeled and cut into 1/2-inch cubes
1 teaspoon curry powder
1/2 teaspoon minced garlic
1 pound sea scallops
1 cup frozen peas
1/4 cup low-fat (1%) milk

Combine clam juice, wine, potatoes, garlic, and curry in a 4-quart pot. Cover pot, and bring mixture to a boil. Reduce heat, and simmer mixture for 10 minutes. Add scallops; simmer until scallops are cooked through, 5 to 10 minutes. Using a slotted spoon, transfer half the mixture to a bowl; keep scallops and potatoes warm.

Using an immersion blender, puree mixture remaining in pot. Stir in peas, milk, and reserved scallops and potatoes. Cook until chowder is hot throughout and peas are tender, about 5 minutes (do not boil), stirring occasionally.

HELPFUL HINT

Halve or quarter large scallops so they're all equal in size and will cook uniformly.

PER SERVING:
Calories: 262
Fat (g): 1.7
Saturated Fat (g): 0.2
Cholesterol (mg): 49
Carbohydrates (g): 32.1
Sodium (mg): 449
Dietary Fiber (g): 4.4

EASY MANHATTAN CLAM CHOWDER

Here's a quick version of the always-popular clam chowder. Marjoram, instead of the usual thyme, gives it a subtle flavor twist.

2   slices turkey bacon, diced
2   medium onions, chopped
2   potatoes, cut into $\frac{1}{2}$-inch cubes
1   carrot, thinly sliced
1   can (15 ounces) diced tomatoes
1   cup clam juice
1   can (6 ounces) minced clams with juice
$\frac{1}{2}$ teaspoon marjoram
$\frac{1}{4}$ teaspoon black pepper

In a 4-quart pot, cook bacon over medium-high heat until it's lightly browned, about 5 minutes. Add onions; sauté until they're translucent, about 5 minutes.

Add potatoes, carrots, tomatoes, and clam juice. Cover pot, and bring soup to a boil. Reduce heat, and simmer mixture until carrots are tender, 15 to 20 minutes. Add clams, marjoram, and pepper. Simmer 4 minutes more.

HELPFUL HINT

In a hurry? Don't bother peeling potatoes for this recipe. Simply scrub them well.

PREPARATION TIME:
10 minutes
COOKING TIME:
35 minutes
SERVINGS: *4*

PER SERVING:
Calories: 128
Fat (g): 2.1
Saturated Fat (g): 0.6
Cholesterol (mg): 5.8
Carbohydrates (g): 25.3
Sodium (mg): 355
Dietary Fiber (g): 4

HALIBUT AND POTATO CHOWDER

This chunky chowder has a thick, flavorful base of pureed vegetables. For a fun change of pace, serve the chowder in a bread bowl. To make such a bowl, start with a round loaf of crusty bread. Then cut off its top, and hollow it out.

PREPARATION TIME:

15 minutes

COOKING TIME:

35 minutes

SERVINGS: *4*

2 slices turkey bacon

1 large onion, chopped

1 celery stalk, chopped

1½ cups clam juice

4 cups peeled and cubed potatoes

1 teaspoon ground savory

1–2 teaspoons Louisiana-style hot-pepper sauce

1 carrot, coarsely shredded

1 pound halibut steak, cut into ¾-inch pieces

1 cup low-fat (1%) milk

Cook bacon in a 4-quart pot over medium-high heat until crisp. Drain bacon on paper towels. Crumble bacon and set it aside.

Add onions and celery to pot; sauté vegetables until they're translucent and tender, about 5 minutes.

Whisk in clam juice. Stir in potatoes. Cover pot and simmer mixture until potatoes are tender, about 15 minutes. Using a slotted spoon, transfer half the vegetables to a bowl; keep them warm.

Using a potato masher or a hand-held immersion blender, puree the vegetables in the pot. Return reserved vegetables to pot. Stir in savory and pepper sauce.

Bring mixture to a simmer and add carrots and halibut. Cook the chowder, covered, until carrots and halibut are done, 3 to 5 minutes. Stir in milk; heat chowder until hot. Divide it among 4 bowls; top each serving with bacon.

In this recipe, I use Crystal's Louisiana hot-pepper sauce, a fairly mild variety. If you choose a different brand—most other sauces have considerably more heat than Crystal's—add it by the dropful, checking nippiness and flavor after each addition.

To remove small bones from halibut, use needle-nose pliers.

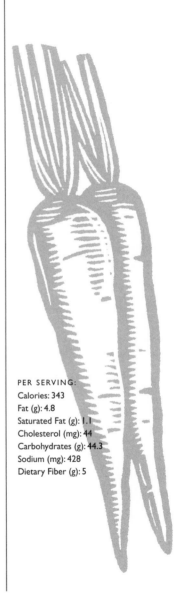

PER SERVING:
Calories: 343
Fat (g): 4.8
Saturated Fat (g): 1.1
Cholesterol (mg): 44
Carbohydrates (g): 44.3
Sodium (mg): 428
Dietary Fiber (g): 5

LIGHTHOUSE CLAM CHOWDER

Looking for a mouth-watering New England-style chowder, one that's creamy and loaded with clams and potatoes? Then you've picked the right recipe, and this one has just 3.9 grams of fat, tops.

PREPARATION TIME:

10 minutes

COOKING TIME:

30 minutes

SERVINGS: 4

1 can (11 ounces) clam juice
2 cans (6½ ounces each) minced clams, drained and juice reserved
2 medium potatoes, cut into ½-inch cubes
1 onion, chopped
1 celery stalk
1½ cups 2% milk
1 slice (1 ounce) lean deli ham, chopped
2 teaspoons Worcestershire sauce
¾ teaspoon thyme leaves

Combine clam juice, reserved clam juice, potatoes, onions, and celery in a 4-quart pot. Cover pot and bring mixture to a boil. Reduce heat and simmer mixture until potatoes are tender, 15 to 20 minutes. Using a slotted spoon, transfer half the vegetables to a bowl; keep them warm.

Using a hand-held immersion blender, puree the vegetables in the pot. Return reserved vegetables to pot. Stir in clams, milk, ham, Worcestershire, and thyme. Heat chowder until it's hot throughout (do not boil), 5 to 10 minutes. Serve immediately.

HELPFUL HINT

To use fresh minced clams instead of the canned variety, alter this recipe as follows: Stir the clams into the puree and cook them for 3 to 4 minutes; then add the milk and remaining ingredients and heat the chowder until it's hot throughout, 5 to 10 minutes.

PER SERVING:
Calories: 305
Fat (g): 3.9
Saturated Fat (g): 1.4
Cholesterol (mg): 72
Carbohydrates (g): 35.5
Sodium (mg): 443
Dietary Fiber (g): 2.8

LOBSTER AND SHRIMP CHOWDER

This singular chowder is elegant enough for a special dinner party, easy enough for a casual supper, and fast enough for a weeknight meal.

2 large Yukon gold potatoes, cut into $\frac{1}{2}$-inch cubes
1 Spanish onion, chopped
1 can (15 ounces) diced tomatoes
1 can (11 ounces) clam juice
$\frac{1}{2}$ pound cooked lobster, cut into small chunks
$\frac{1}{4}$ pound cooked small shrimp
1 teaspoon dried tarragon leaves
1 cup low-fat (1%) milk
$\frac{1}{4}$ cup snipped fresh parsley

Combine potatoes, onions, tomatoes, and clam juice in a 4-quart pot. Cover pot, and bring mixture to a boil. Reduce heat, and simmer mixture until potatoes are tender, about 12 minutes.

Add lobster, shrimp, and tarragon; simmer 5 minutes more. Stir in milk and parsley; heat until hot throughout, about 2 minutes.

HELPFUL HINT

To save time, buy cooked lobster and shrimp in your supermarket's seafood section.

PREPARATION TIME:

10 minutes

COOKING TIME:

25 minutes

SERVINGS: *4*

PER SERVING:
Calories: 314
Fat (g): 2.6
Saturated Fat (g): 0.8
Cholesterol (mg): 230
Carbohydrates (g): 35.3
Sodium (mg): 671
Dietary Fiber (g): 4.1

MEDITERRANEAN FISHERMEN'S STEW

In this simple stew, which nets cod, tomatoes, zucchini, and carrots, canned clam juice makes a quick and easy alternative to homemade fish stock.

PREPARATION TIME:

20 minutes

COOKING TIME:

45 minutes

SERVINGS: **4**

1	teaspoon olive oil
1	large onion, chopped
4	teaspoons minced garlic
1	can (28 ounces) plum tomatoes, cut up
2	medium zucchini, sliced
2	carrots, thinly sliced
1	can (10 ounces) clam juice
$^1\!/_2$–1	teaspoon lemon pepper
1	pound cod, cut into 1-inch cubes
1	tablespoon snipped fresh basil
$^1\!/_2$	cup snipped fresh flat-leaf parsley

Warm oil in a 4-quart pot over medium-high heat for 1 minute. Add onions and garlic; sauté them until they're translucent, about 5 minutes.

Stir in tomatoes, zucchini, carrots, clam juice, and lemon pepper. Cover pot; bring mixture to a boil. Reduce heat; simmer mixture until carrots are tender, 20 to 25 minutes.

Add cod and basil; cook until cod is cooked through, 5 to 10 minutes. Stir in parsley.

HELPFUL HINT

Though you can use either flat-leaf or curly-leaf parsley in this recipe, the flat-leaf variety has slightly more flavor.

PER SERVING:
Calories: 192
Fat (g): 2.8
Saturated Fat (g): 0.4
Cholesterol (mg): 49
Carbohydrates (g): 19.8
Sodium (mg): 292
Dietary Fiber (g): 5.1

MONKFISH-CHEDDAR CHOWDER

One nibble and I was hooked on this rich-tasting, creamy chowder with monkfish, potatoes, and carrots. I think you'll find it irresistible, too.

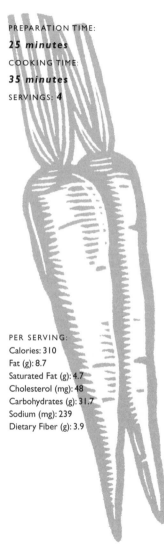

PREPARATION TIME:
25 minutes
COOKING TIME:
35 minutes
SERVINGS: **4**

- 2 teaspoons butter
- 1 medium onion, chopped
- 2 large potatoes (about 1 pound), peeled and cut into $\frac{1}{2}$-inch cubes
- 2 carrots, thinly sliced
- 1 can (14 ounces) fat-free chicken broth
- 1 pound monkfish, membrane removed and flesh cut into $\frac{3}{4}$-inch cubes
- $\frac{1}{2}$ cup skim milk
- $\frac{1}{2}$ cup shredded reduced-sodium Cheddar cheese
- 1 teaspoon Louisiana-style hot-pepper sauce
- 1 tablespoon snipped fresh chives

Melt butter in a 4-quart pot over medium-high heat. Add onions; cook until they're softened. Add potatoes, carrots, and broth. Cover pot, and bring mixture to a boil. Reduce heat, and simmer mixture until potatoes and carrots are tender, about 12 minutes. Using a slotted spoon, transfer 2 cups of vegetables to a bowl; keep them warm.

Using a hand-held immersion blender, puree the vegetables in the pot. Add monkfish. Cover pot, and simmer mixture until monkfish is tender, 5 to 10 minutes. Stir in milk, Cheddar, hot-pepper sauce, and reserved vegetables. Heat chowder until it's hot (do not boil). Top each serving with chives.

HELPFUL HINT

Removing the membrane from monkfish isn't difficult: Simply pull it away from the flesh and use kitchen scissors to cut it.

PER SERVING:
Calories: 310
Fat (g): 8.7
Saturated Fat (g): 4.7
Cholesterol (mg): 48
Carbohydrates (g): 31.7
Sodium (mg): 239
Dietary Fiber (g): 3.9

SALMON AND ROASTED PEPPER CHOWDER

Salmon aficionados take note: In this recipe, salmon is paired with corn and seasoned with jalapeño peppers, cumin, and oregano for a fast and fabulous feast.

PREPARATION TIME:

20 minutes

COOKING TIME:

25 minutes

SERVINGS: *4*

2 cups frozen corn

2 medium potatoes, peeled and cut into $\frac{1}{2}$-inch cubes

2 cups reduced-sodium vegetable broth

2 jalapeño peppers, seeded and minced

2 teaspoons minced garlic

1 teaspoon cumin seeds

1 teaspoon dried oregano

$\frac{3}{4}$ pound salmon steak, bones removed and cut into $1\frac{1}{2}$-inch cubes

1 cup chopped roasted red pepper

1 tablespoon snipped fresh parsley

Combine corn, potatoes, broth, jalapeño peppers, garlic, cumin, oregano, and salmon in a 4-quart pot. Cover pot, and bring mixture to a boil. Reduce heat, and simmer mixture until potatoes are tender and salmon is cooked through, about 20 minutes. Stir in roasted peppers. Top each serving with parsley.

HELPFUL HINT

Here's how to tell if the salmon is cooked through: Gently separate the flesh, using a fork or the tip of a knife. If the fish is done, it will flake easily.

PER SERVING:

Calories: 301

Fat (g): 6.3

Saturated Fat (g): 0.9

Cholesterol (mg): 47

Carbohydrates (g): 41.9

Sodium (mg): 97

Dietary Fiber (g): 5.1

SEAFOOD SAMPLER

Can't decide whether to buy haddock, scallops, or shrimp? Then get some of each and simmer up this sensibly seasoned chowder. It includes favorite vegetables and a little dry white wine. Accompany the chowder with croutons or a chunk of crusty bread.

PREPARATION TIME:

25 minutes

COOKING TIME:

35 minutes

SERVINGS: *4*

1	teaspoon olive oil
1	yellow bell pepper, chopped
1	medium onion, cut into thin wedges
1	can (15 ounces) diced tomatoes
2	medium potatoes, cut into 1/2-inch cubes
1/2	cup dry white wine
1/4	pound shrimp, peeled and deveined
1/4	pound bay scallops
1/2	pound haddock, cut into 1-inch cubes
1	teaspoon herbes de Provence seasoning
1/2	teaspoon celery seeds
1	teaspoon Louisiana-style hot-pepper sauce

Warm oil in a 4-quart pot over medium-high heat for 1 minute. Add peppers and onions; sauté the vegetables until they're lightly browned, about 5 minutes.

Add tomatoes, potatoes, and wine; cook mixture for 10 minutes. Add shrimp, scallops, haddock, herb seasoning, and celery seeds. Cover pot, and simmer mixture until fish is cooked through and potatoes are tender, 10 to 15 minutes. Stir in hot-pepper sauce.

HELPFUL HINTS

Use whole celery seed in this chowder; the ground variety will give the dish a murky look.

If your supermarket doesn't carry herbes de Provence seasoning, substitute Italian herb seasoning.

PER SERVING:
Calories: 237
Fat (g): 2.7
Saturated Fat (g): 0.4
Cholesterol (mg): 76
Carbohydrates (g): 29.3
Sodium (mg): 108
Dietary Fiber (g): 4

SHRIMP AND BABY VEGETABLES

Prep time is short for this stew. It relies on baby vegetables—corn, carrots, and Brussels sprouts—which need no chopping or slicing.

PREPARATION TIME:
10 minutes
COOKING TIME:
30 minutes
SERVINGS: *4*

8 ounces baby carrots
1 can (15 ounces) baby corn, drained
1 large white onion, cut into thin wedges
1 can (16 ounces) stewed tomatoes
$\frac{1}{4}$ pound light smoked sausage, halved lengthwise and sliced $\frac{1}{4}$ inch thick
1 teaspoon chili powder
$\frac{3}{4}$ pound medium shrimp, shelled and deveined
1 cup baby Brussels sprouts, *or* halved larger Brussels sprouts

Combine carrots, corn, onions, tomatoes, sausage, and chili powder in a 4-quart pot. Cover pot, and simmer mixture for 20 minutes.

Stir in shrimp; cook mixture for 5 minutes. Stir in Brussels sprouts; cook stew until shrimp are pink and cooked through and Brussels are tender, about 5 minutes.

HELPFUL HINT

Shrimp is cooked through when it has turned pink, curled up, and looks opaque.

PER SERVING:
Calories: 376
Fat (g): 8.8
Saturated Fat (g): 2.8
Cholesterol (mg): 129
Carbohydrates (g): 51.6
Sodium (mg): 666
Dietary Fiber (g): 9

SHRIMP AND SAUSAGE GUMBO

Okra plays a dual role in this fast-to-make version of the bayou favorite, gumbo: It thickens the stew while giving it a characteristic Creole flavor.

1	cup rice
1	teaspoon butter
1/4	pound turkey sausage, cut lengthwise and thinly sliced
2	cloves garlic, minced
1	red bell pepper, chopped
8	ounces fresh, *or* frozen, okra, sliced
2	cans (14 ounces each) stewed tomatoes
1	dried cayenne pepper, minced
1/2	pound medium shrimp, peeled and deveined

Cook rice according to package directions, omitting salt.

Meanwhile, melt butter in a 4-quart pot over medium-high heat. Add sausage; sauté until it's browned, about 5 minutes. Add garlic and sauté mixture for 30 seconds.

Stir in bell pepper, okra, tomatoes, cayenne, and shrimp. Cover pot, and bring gumbo to a boil. Reduce heat, and simmer gumbo until shrimp is pink and cooked through, about 10 minutes. Serve over rice.

HELPFUL HINT

Let frozen okra thaw, pieces separated, for 5 to 10 minutes before slicing it.

PREPARATION TIME:

20 minutes

COOKING TIME:

20 minutes

SERVINGS: *4*

PER SERVING:
Calories: 390
Fat (g): 5.1
Saturated Fat (g): 1.7
Cholesterol (mg): 107
Carbohydrates (g): 61.7
Sodium (mg): 412
Dietary Fiber (g): 4.3

SPICY CRAB AND SCALLOP CHOWDER

Ladle up some fare with flair: The flavor kick in this seafood chowder comes from pickling spice, which is readily available in supermarkets.

PREPARATION TIME:

10 minutes

COOKING TIME:

20 minutes

SERVINGS: *4*

1	tablespoon butter
1	medium onion, chopped
1	celery stalk, diced
1½	cups clam juice
1	can (14 ounces) stewed tomatoes
2	teaspoons pickling spice
1	can (4 ounces) lump crab meat, drained
½	pound bay scallops
¼	cup half-and-half cream

Melt butter in a 4-quart pot over medium-high heat. Add onions and celery; sauté until they're softened, about 6 minutes. Add clam juice and stewed tomatoes. Place pickling spice in a mesh tea ball or tie it in cheesecloth; add it to mixture.

Simmer mixture for 2 minutes. Stir in crabmeat and scallops; cook the chowder until scallops are done, 6 to 8 minutes. Discard seasonings. Stir in cream; heat chowder until it's hot.

HELPFUL HINT

After adding the cream, heat the soup until it's just hot. Don't let it boil or the cream may curdle.

PER SERVING:
Calories: 188
Fat (g): 6.1
Saturated Fat (g): 3
Cholesterol (mg): 72
Carbohydrates (g): 12.7
Sodium (mg): 697
Dietary Fiber (g): 1.7

THAI-STYLE SHRIMP AND SWEET PEPPERS

This beautiful dish gets its matchless gourmet flavor from shrimp, bok choy, scallions, and Chinese chili sauce. For a different flavor experience, top the dish with chopped, dry-roasted peanuts.

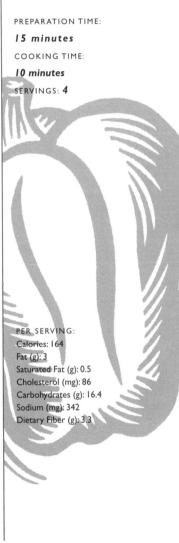

PREPARATION TIME:
15 minutes
COOKING TIME:
10 minutes
SERVINGS: *4*

- 2 cups fat-free chicken broth
- 1/4 cup rice wine vinegar
- 2 tablespoons Chinese chili sauce with garlic
- 1/2 pound medium shrimp, peeled and deveined
- 2 cups chopped bok choy
- 1 medium red bell pepper, cut into thin 1-inch-long strips
- 1 cup sliced scallions
- 4 ounces bean threads, cut into short lengths and soaked in hot water for 10 minutes
- 1 cup bean sprouts

Bring broth, vinegar, and chili sauce to a boil in a 4-quart pot. Add shrimp; simmer mixture for 3 minutes. Add bok choy, peppers, and scallions; simmer mixture until shrimp are done, about 5 minutes.

Stir in bean threads and sprouts; simmer until threads are al dente, about 1 minute.

HELPFUL HINT

You can use either fresh or canned bean sprouts in this recipe. Whichever you choose, rinse and drain them before adding them to the dish.

PER SERVING:
Calories: 164
Fat (g): 3
Saturated Fat (g): 0.5
Cholesterol (mg): 86
Carbohydrates (g): 16.4
Sodium (mg): 342
Dietary Fiber (g): 3.3

presenting
prime
poultry

Cali-Florida Chili

Chicken Athenos with Feta

Chicken Cacciatore with Ziti

Chicken Chowder Hispanola

Chicken Corn Chowder with Sweet Peppers

Chicken in Sauce Provençal

Italian Sausage Stew with Peppers

Lime Chicken with Avocado

Prairie Chili with Chicken

Mesquite Chicken Chili

Moroccan Chicken Stew with Couscous

Home-Style Turkey Stew

Quick Gnocchi Chowder with Smoked Turkey

Old Hickory Chili with White Beans

Roasted Peppers Chili

Sweet Italian Sausage and Fennel Stew

Turkey Sancoche

Turkey-Wild Rice Stew

presenting prime poultry

CALI-FLORIDA CHILI

With this chili, experience a regional "fusion" cuisine that traces its heritage right to the good old U.S.A.

1 teaspoon crushed mixed peppercorns
1 pound boneless, skinless chicken breast, cut into 1-inch cubes
4 cups sliced plum tomatoes
1 cup sun-dried tomatoes, diced
1 cup Zinfandel, *or* other dry red wine
2 dried California chilies, chopped
4 teaspoons chili powder
1 Florida avocado, chopped
2 tablespoons sunflower seeds, toasted
1 cup snipped fresh purple basil

Sprinkle $\frac{1}{2}$ teaspoon peppercorns in a nonstick skillet. Add chicken and sauté until the pieces are lightly browned.

Combine fresh and dried tomatoes, wine, chilies, and chili powder in a 4-quart pot. Add chicken. Cover pot, and bring mixture to a boil. Reduce heat, and simmer mixture for 6 minutes, stirring twice. Uncover pot; simmer mixture 4 minutes more.

Stir in avocado, sunflower seeds, and remaining crushed peppercorns. Serve chili topped with basil.

HELPFUL HINT

For directions on toasting seeds, see "Helpful Hint" under Tenderloin Chili (page 111).

PREPARATION TIME:
15 minutes
COOKING TIME:
20 minutes
SERVINGS: *6*

PER SERVING:
Calories: 331
Fat (g): 9.7
Saturated Fat (g): 1.8
Cholesterol (mg): 64
Carbohydrates (g): 29
Sodium (mg): 115
Dietary Fiber (g): 8.4

CHICKEN ATHENOS WITH FETA

Cinnamon and lemon pair up to give this tomato-based stew the signature flavors of Greek cooking. And classic, crumbly feta cheese tops the dish off with an unexpected salty tang.

PREPARATION TIME:

10 minutes

COOKING TIME:

25 minutes

SERVINGS: *4*

1 teaspoon olive oil

1 pound boneless, skinless chicken breasts, cut into ¾-inch pieces

1 can (14 ounces) stewed tomatoes, cut up

Juice of 1 lemon

1 cinnamon stick

2 teaspoons minced garlic

1 bay leaf

¼ cup dry sherry

8 ounces medium-wide noodles

¼ cup crumbled feta cheese

Warm oil in a 4-quart pot over medium-high heat for 1 minute. Add chicken; sauté until the pieces are lightly browned, about 5 minutes.

Add tomatoes, lemon juice, cinnamon, garlic, bay leaf, and sherry. Cover pot, and bring mixture to a boil. Reduce heat, and simmer stew until chicken is tender and cooked through, about 15 minutes.

Meanwhile, cook noodles according to package directions, omitting salt. Drain the noodles. Toss chicken with noodles, discarding bay leaf and cinnamon. Top each serving with feta.

PER SERVING:

Calories: 511

Fat (g): 9.5

Saturated Fat (g): 3.8

Cholesterol (mg): 111

Carbohydrates (g): 54.3

Sodium (mg): 477

Dietary Fiber (g): 2.8

HELPFUL HINT

Here's how to squeeze the most from a lemon (or lime): Warm the fruit on Medium power in a microwave for 30 to 50 seconds, then roll it on a work surface, pressing it down firmly. Cut and juice the fruit.

CHICKEN CACCIATORE WITH ZITI

Here's a hunter's stew that's just the way you like it: Packed with tender chicken, pungent shallots, mild zucchini, and hearty pasta.

2 teaspoons olive oil

1 pound boneless, skinless chicken breasts, cut into 3/4-inch cubes

1/2 cup chopped shallots

2 cups canned plum tomatoes, cut up

1/4 cup dry red wine

1 small zucchini, sliced

1 teaspoon Italian herb seasoning

4 ounces ziti

PREPARATION TIME:

10 minutes

COOKING TIME:

25 minutes

SERVINGS: **4**

Warm oil in a 4-quart pot over medium-high heat for 1 minute. Add chicken; sauté until the pieces are lightly browned. Add shallots; sauté them until they're translucent.

Add tomatoes, wine, zucchini, and herb seasoning. Cover pot, and bring stew to a boil. Reduce heat, and simmer stew until zucchini are tender, 5 to 10 minutes.

Cook pasta according to package directions, omitting salt. Drain. Stir into chicken mixture.

HELPFUL HINT

No ziti on hand? Then use mostaccioli or rigatoni instead.

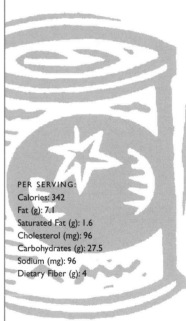

PER SERVING:
Calories: 342
Fat (g): 7.1
Saturated Fat (g): 1.6
Cholesterol (mg): 96
Carbohydrates (g): 27.5
Sodium (mg): 96
Dietary Fiber (g): 4

CHICKEN CHOWDER HISPANOLA

Caribbean fusion cuisine is hot. And so is this enticing chowder that boasts sofrito, a popular Cuban seasoning, and Spanish favorites like pollo (chicken) and olive oil.

PREPARATION TIME:

10 minutes

COOKING TIME:

30 minutes

SERVINGS: **4**

1 teaspoon olive oil

¾ pound boneless, skinless chicken breast, cut into ¾-inch cubes

1 onion, chopped

1 can (15 ounces) garbanzo beans (chick peas), rinsed and drained

1 can (14 ounces) fat-free chicken broth

1 can (15 ounces) whole tomatoes, cut up

2 cups packed fresh spinach leaves

2 tablespoons sofrito sauce

¼ cup slivered almonds, toasted

Warm oil in a 4-quart pot over medium-high heat for 1 minute. Add chicken; sauté until the pieces are lightly browned, about 5 minutes. Add onions; sauté until they're translucent, about 3 minutes.

Add beans, broth, and tomatoes. Cover pot, and bring mixture to a boil. Reduce heat, and simmer mixture 10 minutes. Stir in spinach and sofrito; simmer chowder 10 minutes more.

Divide chowder among 4 bowls. Top each serving with almonds.

HELPFUL HINT

To toast almond slices, place them in a small nonstick skillet over low heat. Warm the almonds until they're lightly browned, 5 to 10 minutes, shaking the skillet occasionally.

PER SERVING:
Calories: 340
Fat (g): 9.3
Saturated Fat (g): 2
Cholesterol (mg): 75
Carbohydrates (g): 27.3
Sodium (mg): 656
Dietary Fiber (g): 8.1

CHICKEN CORN CHOWDER WITH SWEET PEPPERS

Some bright, red bell peppers and a few tablespoons of picante sauce —that's all it takes to transform an ordinary corn chowder into an extra special dish like this one.

1 pound boneless, skinless chicken breast, cut into $1/2$-inch pieces
1 teaspoon olive oil
1 onion, chopped
2 teaspoons minced garlic
2 cups cubed potatoes (about 2 medium)
$1/2$ cup fat-free chicken broth
2 cans (15 ounces each) cream-style corn
1 red bell pepper, chopped
5 tablespoons mild picante sauce
2 teaspoons chopped black olives, for garnish

Warm oil in a 4-quart pot over medium-high heat. Add chicken; sauté until the pieces are browned and cooked through, 7 to 9 minutes. Add onions and garlic, and sauté until the onions are transparent, about 3 minutes. Stir in potatoes and broth, and cover pot. Bring mixture to a boil, lower heat, and simmer until potatoes are tender, about 15 minutes.

Stir in cream-style corn, bell peppers, and picante sauce. Cover and cook over medium heat until hot and slightly thickened, 10 to 15 minutes.

Divide chowder among 4 bowls; top each serving with olives.

HELPFUL HINT

Feeling pressed for time? Then skip peeling the potatoes. Just be sure to scrub them well.

PREPARATION TIME:
10 minutes
COOKING TIME:
45 minutes
SERVINGS: *4*

PER SERVING:
Calories: 356
Fat (g): 5.6
Saturated Fat (g): 1.4
Cholesterol (mg): 95
Carbohydrates (g): 36.9
Sodium (mg): 248
Dietary Fiber (g): 5.8

CHICKEN IN SAUCE PROVENÇAL

Beguile your taste buds with this flavorful entrée. It's bursting with garlic and herb flavors, reminiscent of dishes from southern France's Provence region. A splash of white wine adds to its mystique.

PREPARATION TIME:

10 minutes

COOKING TIME:

30 minutes

SERVINGS: *4*

2	teaspoons olive oil
1	pound boneless, skinless chicken breasts, cut into 3/4-inch cubes
4	teaspoons minced garlic
1	can (28 ounces) whole tomatoes, cut up
4	medium potatoes, peeled and thinly sliced
1	cup mellow white wine
1 1/2	teaspoons herbes de Provence
1/2	cup snipped fresh basil

Warm oil in a 4-quart pot over medium-high heat for 1 minute. Add chicken; sauté until the pieces are lightly browned, 3 to 5 minutes. Stir in garlic; sauté mixture for 1 minute more.

Add tomatoes, potatoes, wine, and seasonings. Cover pot, and bring stew to a boil. Reduce heat, and simmer stew until chicken is cooked through and potatoes are tender, about 20 minutes. Stir in basil.

HELPFUL HINT

Can't find herbes de Provence? It's generally available in the spice section of large supermarkets, but if your grocery doesn't carry it, simply make your own: Whisk together 1/2 teaspoon each of rosemary, marjoram, and thyme.

PER SERVING:
Calories: 342
Fat (g): 7.1
Saturated Fat (g): 1.5
Cholesterol (mg): 95
Carbohydrates (g): 22.3
Sodium (mg): 108
Dietary Fiber (g): 3.2

76

ITALIAN SAUSAGE STEW WITH PEPPERS

Tasters said this stew reminded them of a sassy hot sausage and peppers sandwich. I think you'll agree. For extra flavor depth, top it with grated Romano cheese.

½ pound hot Italian turkey sausage
2 onions, cut into thin wedges
1 cubanel pepper, cut into thin 2-inch-long strips
2 cups fat-free chicken broth
1 can (15 ounces) diced tomatoes
1 zucchini, halved lengthwise and sliced ½ inch thick
4 ounces rigati
3 teaspoons chopped garlic
1½ teaspoons Italian herb seasoning
½ teaspoon crushed red pepper flakes

Cook sausage, onions, and cubanel peppers in a nonstick skillet until sausage is lightly browned. Halve sausage lengthwise, and slice it ½ inch thick. Transfer sausage and vegetables to a 4-quart pot.

Add broth, tomatoes, zucchini, rigati, garlic, herb seasoning, and red pepper. Cover pot, and bring soup to a boil. Reduce heat, and simmer stew until rigati are al dente, 10 to 12 minutes.

HELPFUL HINT

If your supermarket is fresh out of canned diced tomatoes, substitute canned whole tomatoes and cut them up yourself.

PREPARATION TIME:
10 minutes
COOKING TIME:
25 minutes
SERVINGS: **4**

PER SERVING:
Calories: 349
Fat (g): 7.5
Saturated Fat (g): 1.9
Cholesterol (mg): 30
Carbohydrates (g): 51.1
Sodium (mg): 563
Dietary Fiber (g): 5

LIME CHICKEN WITH AVOCADO

Ladle up some great eating with this lively chowder. Lime provides the dominant flavor while tomatoes and avocados contribute crisp color contrasts. Tender rice gives the whole dish a creamy base.

PREPARATION TIME:

15 minutes

COOKING TIME:

25 minutes

SERVINGS: *4*

½ pound boneless, skinless chicken breasts, cut into ¾-inch pieces

½ pound medium shrimp, peeled, deveined, and halved crosswise

2 cans (14 ounces each) fat-free chicken broth

½ cup rice

Juice of 1 lime

⅛ teaspoon celery seeds

4 scallions, sliced

½ teaspoon crushed red pepper flakes

3 plum tomatoes, coarsely chopped

1 teaspoon grated lime peel

1 avocado, cut into ¾-inch pieces

Combine the chicken, shrimp, broth, rice, lime juice, and celery seed in a 4-quart pot. Cover pot, and simmer mixture until chicken and shrimp are cooked through and rice is tender, 15 to 20 minutes.

Stir in scallions, red peppers, tomatoes, and lime peel. Heat chowder for 1 minute. Stir in avocado. Serve chowder immediately.

HELPFUL HINT

When preparing citrus fruit, always grate the peel, *then* juice the pulp. For directions on getting the most juice from a lemon or lime, see "Helpful Hint" under Chicken Athenos with Feta (page 72).

PER SERVING:

Calories: 301

Fat (g): 8.8

Saturated Fat (g): 1.8

Cholesterol (mg): 105

Carbohydrates (g): 28.6

Sodium (mg): 249

Dietary Fiber (g): 4.8

PRAIRIE CHILI WITH CHICKEN

Few dishes have snappier flavor or are simpler to prepare than this six-minute chili. Sporting dried poblanos and a mild picante sauce, it ranks low on the scoville heat scale. Looking for a fiery punch? Then double the red pepper flakes and use a hot picante sauce.

PREPARATION TIME:

5 minutes

COOKING TIME:

10 minutes

SERVINGS: **4**

¾ pound cooked chicken breast, shredded
1 can (14 ounces) stewed tomatoes
1 cup mild picante sauce
2 ancho peppers (dried poblanos), chopped
2 tablespoons dried onion flakes
½ teaspoon crushed red pepper flakes
1 teaspoon paprika
1 teaspoon dried parsley
1 cup fresh bean sprouts

Combine chicken, tomatoes, picante sauce, chopped dried peppers, onions, pepper flakes, and paprika in a 4-quart pot. Cover pot, and bring chili to a boil. Reduce heat, and simmer chili for 5 minutes.

Add parsley and sprouts; simmer chili for 1 minute more.

HELPFUL HINTS

Having trouble getting fresh bean sprouts? Then substitute rinsed and drained canned ones.

To make this chili in a slow cooker: Combine all ingredients except sprouts in an electric slow cooker. Cover cooker and cook chili on Low for 5 to 6 hours. Stir in the sprouts and serve.

PER SERVING:
Calories: 275
Fat (g): 3.5
Saturated Fat (g): 0.9
Cholesterol (mg): 72
Carbohydrates (g): 29.6
Sodium (mg): 318
Dietary Fiber (g): 3.5

MESQUITE CHICKEN CHILI

Looking for a differently delicious Tex-Mex dish—one that will appeal to adventurous and not-so-adventurous palates alike? Quest no more. This fast chili will fill the bill. And it gets its unique essence from mesquite flavoring and tomatillos.

PREPARATION TIME:

15 minutes

COOKING TIME:

20 minutes

SERVINGS: *4*

1 teaspoon olive oil

¾ pound boneless, skinless chicken breasts, cut into ½-inch cubes

1 large onion, chopped

1 can (28 ounces) crushed tomatoes

½ pound tomatillos, husked and coarsely chopped

1 can (15 ounces) small red beans, rinsed and drained

1 poblano pepper, seeded and minced

2 tablespoons chili powder

2 teaspoons minced garlic

1 teaspoon mesquite smoke flavoring

PER SERVING:
Calories: 386
Fat (g): 6.7
Saturated Fat (g): 1.4
Cholesterol (mg): 72
Carbohydrates (g): 45.5
Sodium (mg): 126
Dietary Fiber (g): 13.6

Warm oil in a 4-quart pot over medium-high heat for 1 minute. Add chicken: sauté until the pieces are lightly browned, about 5 minutes. Add onions; cook the mixture until the onions are translucent, about 3 minutes.

Add crushed tomatoes, tomatillos, beans, peppers, chili powder, and garlic. Cover pot, and bring chili to a boil. Reduce heat, and simmer chili for 10 minutes. Stir in smoke flavoring.

HELPFUL HINT

Before chopping or cooking tomatillos, remove their papery husks and rinse them to remove the sticky covering.

MOROCCAN CHICKEN STEW WITH COUSCOUS

Tantalize your taste buds with this extra-easy version of an exotic Middle-Eastern stew. In it, sweet (apricots and currants), savory (tomatoes and garlic), and spicy (cinnamon, coriander, cumin, and cayenne) flavors intermingle to satisfy the most discriminating palate: Yours.

PREPARATION TIME:

15 minutes

COOKING TIME:

30 minutes

SERVINGS: *4*

1 pound boneless, skinless chicken breasts, cut into ¾-inch cubes

¼ teaspoon ground cinnamon

½ teaspoon ground coriander

1 teaspoon olive oil

2 teaspoons minced garlic

½ teaspoon cumin seeds

1 dried cayenne pepper, minced

3 cups stewed tomatoes

¾ cup chopped dried apricots

½ cup dried currants

1 cup couscous

Combine cinnamon and coriander, and sprinkle the spices over the chicken. Warm oil in a 4-quart pot over medium-high heat for 1 minute. Add chicken; sauté until the pieces are lightly browned, about 5 minutes.

Add garlic, cumin, peppers, tomatoes, apricots, and currants. Cover pot, and bring mixture to a boil. Reduce heat, and simmer mixture until chicken is cooked through and apricots are tender, about 15 minutes.

Meanwhile, in a 3-quart saucepan, bring 2 cups water to a boil. Stir in couscous; cover pan and remove from heat. Let sit for 5 minutes. Fluff couscous with a fork. Serve chicken stew over couscous.

HELPFUL HINT

Cutting dried fruit is admittedly sticky business. To make the job easier, use kitchen scissors and flour the blades before cutting the fruit.

To make this stew in a slow cooker or pressure cooker: Season the chicken with cinnamon and coriander, and sauté the pieces in a skillet. Transfer the chicken to an electric slow cooker; add the remaining ingredients except the couscous. Cover the cooker and cook the mixture on Low for 5 to 7 hours. Or transfer the chicken to a pressure cooker. Lock the cooker's lid into place and bring the cooker up to pressure. Cook 5 minutes and quick release the pressure. In either method, cook the couscous as per recipe directions.

PER SERVING:
Calories: 560
Fat (g): 5.9
Saturated Fat (g): 1.4
Cholesterol (mg): 96
Carbohydrates (g): 82.4
Sodium (mg): 472
Dietary Fiber (g): 5.5

HOME-STYLE TURKEY STEW

Here's a thymely stew that's chockablock with tasty vegetables—mushrooms, potatoes, carrots, and peas—and ready to serve after just 25 minutes of cooking.

2 teaspoons olive oil

¾ pound boneless, skinless turkey breast, cut into ¾-inch cubes

2 medium onions, cut into wedges

4 ounces mushrooms, halved

2 carrots, cut into ½-inch slices

2 potatoes, cut into ¾-inch cubes

1 can (14 ounces) fat-free chicken broth

¾ teaspoon celery seeds

1¼ teaspoons dried thyme leaves

1 cup frozen peas

Warm oil in a 4-quart pot over medium-high heat for 1 minute. Add turkey, onions, and mushrooms; sauté mixture until onions are translucent, about 8 minutes.

Add carrots, potatoes, broth, celery seeds, and thyme. Cover pot, and bring mixture to a boil. Reduce heat, and simmer mixture until turkey and carrots are tender, about 12 minutes. Stir in peas; cook stew until peas are done, 3 to 4 minutes.

HELPFUL HINT

For a thicker broth, stir 4 tablespoons instant flour into the stew just before serving; cook until thickened, 2 to 3 minutes, stirring occasionally.

For a peppery zing, add ½ teaspoon freshly ground black pepper.

To cook this stew in a slow cooker or pressure cooker: Sauté the turkey, onions, and mushrooms in a skillet. Transfer the mixture to an electric slow cooker. Add all remaining ingredients except the peas. Cover the cooker and cook the stew on Low for 5 to 7 hours. Or transfer the mixture to a pressure cooker. Lock the cooker's lid into place and bring the cooker up to pressure over medium-high or high heat. Cook the stew for 6 minutes and quick-release the pressure. In either method, stir in the peas. Cook the stew until the peas are done.

PREPARATION TIME:

15 minutes

COOKING TIME:

25 minutes

SERVINGS: 4

PER SERVING:
Calories: 290
Fat (g): 3.4
Saturated Fat (g): 0.6
Cholesterol (mg): 71
Carbohydrates (g): 30
Sodium (mg): 135
Dietary Fiber (g): 6

QUICK GNOCCHI CHOWDER WITH SMOKED TURKEY

Gnocchi, Italian for "dumplings," are usually topped with butter and Parmesan cheese and served as a side dish. Here, they're the main attraction in a stew that's loaded with broccoli, cauliflower, and smoked deli turkey as well. Magnifico!

PREPARATION TIME:

15 minutes

COOKING TIME:

10 minutes

SERVINGS: 4

1 cup fat-free chicken broth

1 can (15 ounces) crushed tomatoes

¾ pound smoked deli turkey, cut into ½-inch cubes

3 cups (about 1 pound) frozen gnocchi pasta

1 teaspoon poultry seasoning

2 cups broccoli florets

2 cups cauliflower florets

½ cup snipped fresh basil

¼ cup grated provolone cheese

Combine broth, tomatoes, turkey, gnocchi, and seasoning in a 4-quart pot. Cover pot, and simmer mixture for 5 minutes. Stir in broccoli and cauliflower; simmer for 5 minutes more. Stir in basil and provolone.

HELPFUL HINT

Ask the attendant at the deli counter to slice the turkey ½ inch thick. That way, when cubing the meat, you'll have fewer cuts to make.

PER SERVING:
Calories: 240
Fat (g): 7.3
Saturated Fat (g): 4.3
Cholesterol (mg): 65
Carbohydrates (g): 19.9
Sodium (mg): 340
Dietary Fiber (g): 2.9

OLD HICKORY CHILI WITH WHITE BEANS

Holy smokes! This quick hickory-smoked turkey chili is made without wood chips or a grill. The cook's flavor trick: Hickory smoke concentrate.

$\frac{1}{2}$ pound ground turkey breast
 1 cup chopped Spanish onion
 1 cup medium-hot salsa
 1 can (15 ounces) diced tomatoes
 1 can (15 ounces) white kidney beans, rinsed and drained
 2 tablespoons chili powder
 1 tablespoon white wine vinegar
 2 tablespoons snipped fresh cilantro
 1 teaspoon hickory smoke flavoring

Cook turkey in a 4-quart pot until it is crumbly and no longer pink, stirring often. Add onions and sauté mixture until the onions are translucent.

Add salsa, tomatoes, beans, chili powder, and vinegar. Cover pot, and bring chili to a boil. Reduce heat, and simmer the mixture for 10 minutes. Stir in cilantro and smoke flavoring.

HELPFUL HINT

Because white wine vinegar and white distilled vinegar have such distinctly different tastes, never switch the two in a recipe. The wine variety is pleasantly pungent; the distilled one, which is made from grain-alcohol, tastes harsh.

PREPARATION TIME:
10 minutes
COOKING TIME:
20 minutes
SERVINGS: *4*

PER SERVING:
Calories: 248
Fat (g): 4.3
Saturated Fat (g): 0.7
Cholesterol (mg): 47
Carbohydrates (g): 28.6
Sodium (mg): 88
Dietary Fiber (g): 7.1

ROASTED PEPPERS CHILI

Here's a mild-mannered dish with a lean and healthful profile. For crunch, serve it topped with broken baked tortilla chips.

PREPARATION TIME:
10 minutes
COOKING TIME:
20 minutes
SERVINGS: **4**

$\frac{1}{2}$	pound ground turkey breast
I	cup chopped red onion
I	can (15 ounces) stewed tomatoes
I	can (15 ounces) black beans, rinsed and drained
I	tablespoon chili powder
$\frac{1}{2}$	teaspoon cumin
$\frac{1}{4}$	teaspoon allspice
I	small jalapeño pepper, seeded and minced
$\frac{1}{2}$	cup chopped roasted red peppers

Cook turkey in a 3-quart pot until it's crumbly and no longer pink, about 5 minutes, stirring often. Add onions; sauté mixture until the onions are translucent, about 3 minutes.

Add tomatoes, beans, chili powder, cumin, allspice, and jalapeño peppers; cook chili for 10 minutes. Stir in roasted peppers.

HELPFUL HINT

To make your own baked tortilla chips, slice I or 2 tortillas into I-inch-wide strips. Transfer them to a baking sheet and mist them with olive oil spray. Broil until the strips are crisp and lightly browned, 3 to 5 minutes.

PER SERVING:
Calories: 271
Fat (g): 1.9
Saturated Fat (g): 0.4
Cholesterol (mg): 47
Carbohydrates (g): 36.8
Sodium (mg): 66
Dietary Fiber (g): 12.5

SWEET ITALIAN SAUSAGE AND FENNEL STEW

A perennial favorite—sweet Italian sausage—perks up this stew of squash, parsnips, and Brussels sprouts. To spice things up a bit more, replace the sweet sausage with the hot variety.

PREPARATION TIME:
25 minutes
COOKING TIME:
35 minutes
SERVINGS: **4**

- ¾ pound sweet Italian turkey sausage
- 1 medium onion, cut into wedges
- 1 can (16 ounces) diced tomatoes
- 1 cup fat-free chicken broth
- 1 pound butternut squash, peeled and cut into ¾-inch cubes
- 2 parsnips, peeled and cut into 2-inch-long sticks
- 1 fennel bulb, trimmed and cut into ½-inch slices
- 12 Brussels sprouts, halved
- ½ teaspoon crushed red pepper flakes
- 1 teaspoon Italian herb seasoning

Cook sausage in a nonstick skillet over medium-high heat for 10 minutes. Add onions; sauté until they're translucent, about 3 minutes. Transfer onions to a 4-quart pot. Slice sausage; add it to the pot.

Stir in tomatoes, broth, squash, parsnips, and fennel. Cover pot, and bring mixture to a boil. Reduce heat, and simmer mixture for 17 minutes. Stir in Brussels, pepper, and herb seasoning. Cook until Brussels are tender, 4 to 5 minutes.

HELPFUL HINTS

When trimming the fennel bulb, discard the stems, leaves, and core.

To cook the stew in a slow cooker or pressure cooker: Sauté the sausage and onions in a skillet according to recipe directions. Transfer them to an electric slow cooker. Stir in tomatoes, broth, squash, parsnips, and fennel. Cover the cooker and cook stew on Low for 5 to 7 hours. Or transfer the sausage and onions to a pressure cooker. Stir in tomatoes, broth, squash, parsnips, and fennel. Lock the cooker's lid into place and bring cooker up to pressure. Cook the stew for 6 to 8 minutes, and quick-release the pressure. In either method, stir in the Brussels, pepper, and herb seasoning last, and cook the stew until the Brussels are tender.

PER SERVING:
Calories: 320
Fat (g): 7.8
Saturated Fat (g): 2.2
Cholesterol (mg): 53
Carbohydrates (g): 44.2
Sodium (mg): 678
Dietary Fiber (g): 12.2

TURKEY SANCOCHE

Hailing from Latin America, sancoche is a hearty stew of meats, fish, vegetables, and seasonings. This one-pot version, which is topped with toasted cashews, features turkey, winter vegetables, and black beans. Annatto provides the warm orange-yellow color.

PREPARATION TIME:

20 minutes

COOKING TIME:

25 minutes

SERVINGS: **4**

1 pound boneless, skinless turkey breast, cut into ¾-inch cubes
1 sweet potato, peeled and cut into ¾-inch cubes
1 potato, peeled and cut into ¾-inch cubes
1 butternut squash, peeled and cut into ¾-inch cubes
1 onion, chopped
1 can (15 ounces) black beans, rinsed and drained
1 can (14 ounces) fat-free chicken broth
1 jalapeño pepper, seeded and minced
1 teaspoon ground annatto
1 teaspoon cumin seeds, toasted
¼ cup coarsely chopped cashews, toasted

Combine turkey, sweet potatoes, potatoes, squash, onions, beans, broth, peppers, annatto, and cumin seeds in a 4-quart pot. Cover pot, and simmer mixture until turkey is tender and cooked through and vegetables are tender, about 20 minutes. Top each serving with cashews.

HELPFUL HINTS

To find annatto, which is available as whole seeds, look in your supermarket's spice or ethnic section. Use a mortar and pestle or an electric spice grinder to grind the seeds. *To chop cashews,* use a chef's knife and cutting board. *To toast seeds and nuts,* follow the directions in "Helpful Hints" under the recipes for Chicken Chowder Hispanola (page 74) and Tenderloin Chili (page 111). *To cook this stew in a slow cooker or pressure cooker:* Combine the turkey, sweet potatoes, potatoes, squash, onions, beans, broth, peppers, annato, and cumin in either an electric slow cooker or a pressure cooker. Cover the slow cooker and cook the stew on Low for 5 to 7 hours. Or lock the lid into position on the pressure cooker, and bring cooker up to pressure over medium-high to high heat. Cook the stew for 10 minutes and quick-release the pressure. Top each serving with cashews.

PER SERVING:
Calories: 522
Fat (g): 5.8
Saturated Fat (g): 1.3
Cholesterol (mg): 94
Carbohydrates (g): 68.4
Sodium (mg): 147
Dietary Fiber (g): 17.5

TURKEY-WILD RICE STEW

Get ready to dine on the wild side; the wild side of rice, that is. Actually, wild rice isn't a rice at all. It is a long-grain marsh grass that grows in the northern Great Lakes region. In this recipe, I've combined wild rice with another native American food, turkey, to create a super stick-to-your-ribs supper.

PREPARATION TIME:
10 minutes
COOKING TIME:
50 minutes
SERVINGS: **4**

1 teaspoon olive oil
1 pound turkey breast, cut into $\frac{1}{2}$-inch cubes
1 onion, finely chopped
3 cups fat-free chicken broth
$\frac{1}{2}$ cup wild rice
2 carrots, thinly sliced
2 cups chopped broccoli florets
1 tablespoon snipped fresh sage

Warm oil in a 4-quart pot over medium-high heat for 1 minute. Add turkey, and sauté until the pieces are lightly browned and cooked through. Add onions; cook mixture until the onions are translucent (do not brown them), about 4 minutes.

Stir in broth, wild rice, and carrots. Cover pot, and bring mixture to a boil. Reduce heat, and simmer until rice is tender, about 45 minutes.

Stir in broccoli and sage; simmer stew until broccoli is tender, 3 to 5 minutes.

HELPFUL HINT

Supermarket's out of fresh sage? Then substitute 1 teaspoon dried sage leaves.

PER SERVING:
Calories: 353
Fat (g): 2.7
Saturated Fat (g): 0.5
Cholesterol (mg): 94
Carbohydrates (g): 38.2
Sodium (mg): 176
Dietary Fiber (g): 7.3

brazenly beef and other meats

Big Red Chili

Chili con Carne Burritos

Chili Tacos

Corned Beef and Red Cabbage Dinner

Five-Spice Beef

Meatballs and Corkscrew Pasta

Paprika-Sirloin Stew with Sour Cream

Quick Beef Goulash

Steak and Sweet Potato Stew

Teriyaki Beef with Broccoli

Traditional Beef Stew

Poblano Veal Chili

Veal Sauvignon with Swiss Chard

Hearty Rosemary Lamb with Sweet Potatoes

Lamb and Turnip Stew with Cilantro

New England Boiled Dinner

Lightning-Fast Chili

Pork Tenderloin with Gremolata

Tenderloin Chili

brazenly beef and other meats

BIG RED CHILI

This spicy chili with red onions, red kidney beans, and red bell peppers puts a whole new light on "seeing red."

PREPARATION TIME:

10 minutes

COOKING TIME:

40 minutes

SERVINGS: *4*

½ pound ground sirloin
1 large red onion, chopped
3 cups crushed tomatoes
1 can (15 ounces) red kidney beans, rinsed and drained
2 tablespoons red wine vinegar
2 tablespoons chili powder
¼ teaspoon allspice
⅔ cup medium-hot picante sauce
1 large red bell pepper, chopped

In a 4-quart pot, cook sirloin until it's crumbly and no longer pink, about 5 minutes, stirring often and draining off fat as necessary. Add onions, and sauté mixture until the onions are translucent.

Add tomatoes, beans, vinegar, chili powder, and allspice. Cover pot, and bring mixture to a boil. Reduce heat; and simmer mixture for 20 minutes.

Stir in picante sauce and bell pepper, and simmer chili for 10 minutes more.

HELPFUL HINT

To crumble the sirloin (or any other ground meat), stir it frequently when it begins to cook.

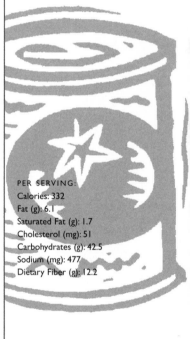

PER SERVING:
Calories: 332
Fat (g): 6.1
Saturated Fat (g): 1.7
Cholesterol (mg): 51
Carbohydrates (g): 42.5
Sodium (mg): 477
Dietary Fiber (g): 12.2

CHILI CON CARNE BURRITOS

Okay, so I'm biased. But this eight-ingredient chili makes a knockout burrito filling that's just about the tastiest I've ever had. Fresh cilantro and an ancho, a dried hot pepper, boost the chili flavor to a high level.

PREPARATION TIME:

10 minutes

COOKING TIME:

30 minutes

SERVINGS: *4*

¾ pound ground sirloin

1 cup chopped onions

1 can (15 ounces) diced tomatoes

1 ancho pepper, chopped

1 tablespoon chili powder

1 teaspoon ground cumin

¼ cup snipped fresh cilantro

4 flour tortillas, warmed according to package directions

In a large nonstick skillet, sauté sirloin until it's crumbly and no longer pink, about 5 minutes, stirring often and draining off fat as necessary. Add onions, and sauté mixture until the onions are translucent, about 3 minutes.

Add tomatoes, ancho peppers, chili powder, and cumin. Bring mixture to a boil. Reduce heat, and simmer chili, uncovered, until it's hot and thickened, about 20 minutes.

Stir in cilantro. Spoon a quarter of chili down the center of each tortilla. Roll up and serve immediately.

HELPFUL HINTS

Why warm tortillas? So they will fold and roll without cracking. If package directions aren't available, here's what to do: Wrap tortillas in foil and place them in a 300° oven for 4 to 5 minutes.

Can't locate an ancho pepper? Use a dried cayenne instead.

PER SERVING:

Calories: 346
Fat (g): 9.8
Saturated Fat (g): 2.9
Cholesterol (mg): 76
Carbohydrates (g): 32.3
Sodium (mg): 258
Dietary Fiber (g): 5.7

CHILI TACOS

Have some fun with this chili dish: Serve it in warm taco shells and, if you want, garnish each taco with some shredded cheese, lettuce, and prepared salsa.

1/4 pound ground round
1 medium onion, chopped
2 teaspoons minced garlic
1 can (15 ounces) crushed tomatoes
2 cups fat-free refried beans
1 tablespoon chili powder
1/4 teaspoon allspice
1 dried cayenne pepper, seeded and minced
8 reduced-sodium taco shells, warmed according to package directions

In a large, nonstick skillet, cook beef until it's crumbly and no longer pink, about 3 minutes, stirring often. Add onions and garlic; sauté until onions are translucent.

Stir in tomatoes, beans, chili powder, allspice, and cayenne. Simmer the chili until it's hot and flavors are blended, 10 to 15 minutes. Spoon into shells.

HELPFUL HINT

Canned reduced-fat and fat-free refried beans are available in most of the large supermarkets.

PREPARATION TIME:

10 minutes

COOKING TIME:

25 minutes

SERVINGS: *4*

PER SERVING:
Calories: 249
Fat (g): 7.5
Saturated Fat (g): 2.2
Cholesterol (mg): 24
Carbohydrates (g): 32.2
Sodium (mg): 480
Dietary Fiber (g): 7.1

CORNED BEEF AND RED CABBAGE DINNER

Don't wait until St. Patrick's Day to enjoy this luck-of-the-Irish stew. It's fast. It's easy. It's delicious.

PREPARATION TIME:

15 minutes

COOKING TIME:

20 minutes

SERVINGS: *4*

¾ pound deli corned beef, cut into ½-inch cubes

4 red potatoes, cut into ½-inch cubes

1 can (14 ounces) fat-free chicken broth

1 tablespoon apple cider vinegar

1 teaspoon pickling spice, placed in a mesh tea ball or tied in cheesecloth

1 pound red cabbage, coarsely sliced

Combine corned beef, potatoes, broth, vinegar, and pickling spice in a 4-quart pot. Cover pot, and bring mixture to a boil. Reduce heat, and simmer mixture for 12 minutes.

Add cabbage; cook stew until the cabbage is tender, 3 to 5 minutes. Serve dinner immediately.

HELPFUL HINTS

To cube the beef quickly, ask the deli counter attendant to slice the beef ½ inch thick. Stack the slices and make crosswise and lengthwise cuts through all layers at once.

To slice cabbage fast, halve it through the core, then place each half, cut-side down, on a cutting board. In each half, make a cut on either side of the core to form a V-shaped wedge. Discard the cores and slice the halves as desired.

PER SERVING:
Calories: 247
Fat (g): 3.5
Saturated Fat (g): 1.2
Cholesterol (mg): 34
Carbohydrates (g): 34.7
Sodium (mg): 620
Dietary Fiber (g): 5.2

FIVE-SPICE BEEF

Here's a simple-to-make stew with lots of Asian-style zing—thanks to five-spice powder and Chinese chili sauce.

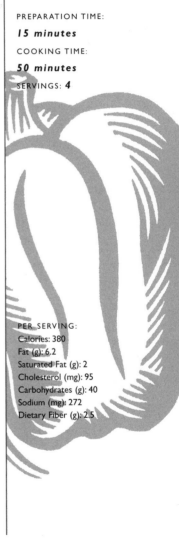

PREPARATION TIME:
15 minutes
COOKING TIME:
50 minutes
SERVINGS: **4**

1 pound round steak, cut into thin 1-inch-long strips
1 cup orange juice
1 cup fat-free beef broth
1 tablespoon teriyaki sauce
1 $\frac{1}{4}$ teaspoons five-spice powder
1 onion, cut into thin wedges
4 ounces bean thread noodles
1 red bell pepper, thinly sliced
1 teaspoon Chinese chili sauce with garlic
2 cups coarsely sliced napa cabbage

Combine beef, orange juice, broth, teriyaki sauce, five-spice powder, and onions in a 4-quart pot. Cover pot, and bring mixture to a boil. Reduce heat, and simmer mixture until beef is tender, about 30 minutes.

Meanwhile, soak bean threads in hot water to cover in a large bowl for 15 minutes.

Stir bell peppers, chili sauce, and cabbage into beef mixture; cook for 3 minutes.

Drain noodles. Stir them into beef stew; cook for 2 minutes more.

HELPFUL HINTS

Having trouble finding bean threads? Check for them in the ethnic section of your supermarket and look under these names: cellophane noodles, glass noodles, and Chinese vermicelli.

Prefer mild dishes? Then use less Chinese chili sauce; it's got quite a bit of nip.

PER SERVING:
Calories: 380
Fat (g): 6.2
Saturated Fat (g): 2
Cholesterol (mg): 95
Carbohydrates (g): 40
Sodium (mg): 272
Dietary Fiber (g): 2.5

MEATBALLS AND CORKSCREW PASTA

Here, onion-and-cheese-seasoned meatballs combine with vegetables and tri-color pasta for a delectable one-dish dinner on the double.

PREPARATION TIME:

30 minutes

COOKING TIME:

40 minutes

SERVINGS: **4**

$^1\!/_2$ pound ground round

1 egg white, lightly beaten

$^1\!/_2$ cup quick oats

3 tablespoons minced dried onions

2 teaspoons Italian herb seasoning

$^1\!/_2$ cup grated Romano cheese

1 can (15 ounces) plum tomatoes, cut up

3 cans (14 ounces each) fat-free beef broth

4 ounces tri-color corkscrew pasta

2 cups small broccoli florets

Combine beef, egg white, oats, 2 teaspoons onions, $^1\!/_2$ teaspoon herb seasoning, and Romano in a bowl. Shape mixture into 16 meatballs (1-inch diameter). Heat a nonstick skillet over medium-high heat for 1 minute. Add meatballs and cook them until they're brown on all sides, about 10 minutes.

Meanwhile, combine tomatoes, broth, remaining onions, and remaining seasoning in a 4-quart pot. Add meatballs. Cover pot and bring mixture to a boil. Reduce heat and simmer mixture for 5 minutes.

Stir in pasta and cook stew for 5 minutes. Stir in broccoli; cook stew until pasta is al dente and broccoli is tender.

HELPFUL HINT

Be sure to form *firm* meatballs; loosely shaped ones may fall apart during cooking.

PER SERVING:

Calories: 360

Fat (g): 7.5

Saturated Fat (g): 3.1

Cholesterol (mg): 56

Carbohydrates (g): 39.3

Sodium (mg): 379

Dietary Fiber (g): 4.7

PAPRIKA-SIRLOIN STEW WITH SOUR CREAM

Imagine tender beef, Italian green beans, and red potatoes cloaked in a heavenly paprika-spiked sour cream sauce. And suppose that such a beef dinner could be ready to eat in about 30 minutes. Daydream no more. Here's the real meal.

PREPARATION TIME:

10 minutes

COOKING TIME:

30 minutes

SERVINGS: *4*

 1 cup fat-free beef broth
 2 cups Italian flat green beans
 ¾ pound red potatoes, cut into ½-inch cubes
 2 bay leaves
 ¾ pound sirloin steak, cut into very thin 1-inch-long strips
 1 cup pearl onions
 1 can (15 ounces) diced tomatoes
 1 tablespoon paprika
 ½ cup nonfat sour cream

Combine broth, beans, potatoes, and bay leaves in a 4-quart pot. Cover pot, and bring mixture to a boil. Reduce heat, and simmer mixture until vegetables are tender, about 10 minutes.

Meanwhile, sauté beef and onions in a large nonstick skillet until beef is lightly browned, about 8 minutes. Transfer to pot containing beans and potatoes.

Add tomatoes and paprika; simmer 5 minutes. Stir in sour cream; cook stew until it's hot throughout and slightly thickened.

HELPFUL HINT

If the steak and onions start to stew in their own juices instead of sautéing, turn up the heat and use a paper towel to blot up the unwanted liquid.

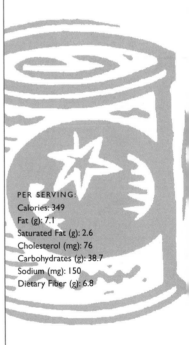

PER SERVING:
Calories: 349
Fat (g): 7.1
Saturated Fat (g): 2.6
Cholesterol (mg): 76
Carbohydrates (g): 38.7
Sodium (mg): 150
Dietary Fiber (g): 6.8

QUICK BEEF GOULASH

In Hungary, this paprika-seasoned stew is called gulyàs, and it's often served with a dollop of sour cream. This fast version includes beef, mushrooms, tomatoes, onions, and cabbage.

PREPARATION TIME:

15 minutes

REFRIGERATION TIME:

55 minutes

SERVINGS: **4**

1	teaspoon olive oil
¾	pound beef bottom round roast, trimmed of fat and cut into ¾-inch cubes
3	large onions, cut into thin wedges
1	cup chopped portobello mushrooms
1	can (14 ounces) diced tomatoes
1	tablespoon paprika
1	teaspoon cocoa
2	cups coarsely sliced cabbage
8	ounces medium-wide noodles
1	tablespoon caraway seeds

Warm oil in a 4-quart pot over medium-high heat for 1 minute. Add beef; sauté until the pieces are browned, about 5 minutes. Add onions and mushrooms; sauté mixture for 5 minutes more.

Add tomatoes, paprika, and cocoa. Cover pot, and bring mixture to a boil. Reduce heat, and simmer mixture 45 minutes. Stir in cabbage; cook stew for 5 minutes more.

Meanwhile, cook noodles according to package directions, omitting salt. Drain the noodles.

Stir caraway into goulash; serve goulash over hot noodles.

PER SERVING:
Calories: 470
Fat (g): 9
Saturated Fat (g): 2.5
Cholesterol (mg): 67
Carbohydrates (g): 62.4
Sodium (mg): 112
Dietary Fiber (g): 5.5

HELPFUL HINT

Egg noodles, as the name suggests, have whole eggs in them; pastas, such as macaroni and spaghetti, don't. If you prefer not to use egg noodles, serve the goulash over linguine or fettuccini.

STEAK AND SWEET POTATO STEW

Apples give this hearty stew a touch of sweetness while savory brings flavor hints of thyme and mint. Enjoy it in the fall when apples are at their peak.

1 pound round steak, cut into ¾-inch cubes
¼ cup flour
1 teaspoon olive oil
1 large onion, cut into thin wedges
1¾ cups fat-free beef broth
1¼ pounds sweet potatoes, peeled and cut into ½-inch cubes
1 teaspoon dried savory leaves
¼ teaspoon lemon pepper
1 pound McIntosh apples, cut into 1-inch cubes
1½ cups frozen peas

PREPARATION TIME:
15 minutes
COOKING TIME:
55 minutes
SERVINGS: *4*

Dredge beef in flour. Warm oil in a 4-quart pot over medium-high heat for 1 minute. Add beef and onions; cook until meat is browned, adding broth as necessary to prevent beef from sticking.

Add remaining broth. Cover pot, and bring mixture to a boil. Reduce heat, and simmer mixture for 30 minutes. Stir in sweet potatoes, savory, and pepper. Simmer mixture until potatoes are tender, 10 to 12 minutes.

Stir in apples and peas; cook stew until peas are tender, about 5 minutes.

HELPFUL HINTS

Once cut, apples oxidize, or turn brown. To slow the process, cut them right before use and dip pieces into lemon juice.

In this recipe, skip peeling the apples. With their skins on, they'll add a splash of red to the stew.

PER SERVING:
Calories: 366
Fat (g): 6.2
Saturated Fat (g): 1.2
Cholesterol (mg): 18
Carbohydrates (g): 66
Sodium (mg): 181
Dietary Fiber (g): 10

TERIYAKI BEEF WITH BROCCOLI

The flavors in this tantalizing stew—gingerroot, onion, broccoli, beef, teriyaki, Chinese wheat noodles—remind me of a favorite rapid-fire stir-fry. And like a stir-fry, this stew is a complete meal in itself.

PREPARATION TIME:
20 minutes
COOKING TIME:
45 minutes
SERVINGS: 4

2	teaspoons olive oil
$\frac{1}{2}$	pound beef round roast, cut into thin strips
1	onion, cut into thin wedges
$1\frac{1}{2}$	cups fat-free beef broth
2	tablespoons low-sodium teriyaki sauce
1	tablespoon minced gingerroot
2	carrots, thinly sliced
2	cups broccoli florets
8	ounces Chinese wheat noodles

Warm oil in a 4-quart pot over medium-high heat for 1 minute. Add beef and onions, and sauté mixture until beef is lightly browned, about 5 minutes.

Stir in broth, teriyaki sauce, and gingerroot. Cover pot, and bring mixture to a boil. Reduce heat, and simmer mixture until beef is tender, about 20 minutes.

Stir in carrots; simmer mixture until carrots are crisp-tender, about 12 minutes. Stir in broccoli; simmer stew until broccoli is tender, about 3 minutes.

Meanwhile, cook noodles according to package directions, omitting salt. Drain the noodles, and toss them with stew.

HELPFUL HINT

Slicing and cubing raw meats and poultry is easiest when these products are icy cold, almost frozen. So if they're frozen, don't completely thaw them before cutting. Or if they're not frozen, place them in the freezer for 20 to 30 minutes before you start cutting.

PER SERVING:
Calories: 467
Fat (g): 8.4
Saturated Fat (g): 1.8
Cholesterol (mg): 38
Carbohydrates (g): 69.9
Sodium (mg): 454
Dietary Fiber (g): 9.9

TRADITIONAL BEEF STEW

I remember my mother's home-style beef stew: It had tender beef, carrots, and potatoes in a rich, dark gravy. And it took hours to cook. Here's a simpler, faster version with all the great familiar flavors.

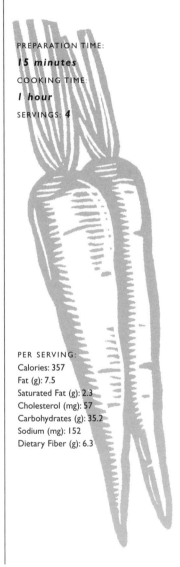

PREPARATION TIME:
15 minutes
COOKING TIME:
1 hour
SERVINGS: **4**

1	teaspoon olive oil
¾	pound round roast, cut into thin, short strips
2	onions, cut into wedges
1½	cups fat-free beef broth
½	cup dry red wine
1	teaspoon cocoa
2	medium potatoes, cut into ½-inch cubes
3	carrots, cut into ½-inch slices
2	cups cut wax beans
½	teaspoon black pepper

Warm oil in a 4-quart pot over medium-high heat for 1 minute. Add beef and onions; sauté mixture until the beef is lightly browned, about 6 minutes. Add broth, wine, and cocoa. Cover pot, and bring mixture to a boil. Reduce heat, and simmer mixture for 25 minutes.

Add potatoes, carrots, and beans; simmer until vegetables are tender, 20 to 25 minutes. Stir in pepper.

HELPFUL HINTS

If you prefer a thick broth, simply stir 1 tablespoon instant flour into the fully cooked stew; cook the stew until the broth thickens, 2 to 5 minutes more.

To prepare this stew in either a slow cooker or pressure cooker: Sauté the beef and onions in a skillet. Then transfer them to an electric slow cooker. Add the remaining ingredients. Cover cooker and cook the stew on Low until the meat and vegetables are tender, 8 to 9 hours. Or transfer beef and onions to a pressure cooker. Lock the cooker's lid into place, and bring the cooker up to pressure over medium-high or high heat. Cook the stew 35 minutes and let pressure drop naturally.

PER SERVING:
Calories: 357
Fat (g): 7.5
Saturated Fat (g): 2.3
Cholesterol (mg): 57
Carbohydrates (g): 35.2
Sodium (mg): 152
Dietary Fiber (g): 6.3

POBLANO VEAL CHILI

Ground veal, a poblano chili, and a store-bought seasoning mix make this fast-track chili an instant favorite.

PREPARATION TIME:
10 minutes
COOKING TIME:
30 minutes
SERVINGS: *4*

1   pound lean ground veal
1   large onion, chopped
1   celery stalk, chopped
2   cups crushed tomatoes
1   can (14 ounces) Great Northern beans, rinsed and drained
1   package (1 $\frac{1}{4}$ ounces) chili seasoning mix
1   poblano pepper, seeded and chopped

Cook veal over medium heat in a 4-quart pot until crumbly and no longer pink, about 8 minutes, stirring often and draining off fat. Add onions and celery; sauté them until they're translucent.

Stir in tomatoes, beans, seasoning mix, and poblano peppers. Cover pot, and bring mixture to a boil. Reduce heat, and simmer mixture 15 minutes.

HELPFUL HINT

Wear rubber gloves when seeding and chopping chili peppers. Capsaicin, the substance responsible for peppers' tasty zing, can sting your skin. Capsaicin is found mostly in peppers' seeds and membranes.

PER SERVING:
Calories: 373
Fat (g): 8.9
Saturated Fat (g): 2.8
Cholesterol (mg): 124
Carbohydrates (g): 35.3
Sodium (mg): 213
Dietary Fiber (g): 12

VEAL SAUVIGNON WITH SWISS CHARD

Delight your taste buds, and those of family and guests as well, with this sophisticated stew. It's a gourmet experience with melt-in-your-mouth veal, tender cauliflower florets, dry white wine, and ziti pasta.

PREPARATION TIME:

15 minutes

COOKING TIME:

15 minutes

SERVINGS: *4*

2	teaspoons olive oil
1/4	teaspoon freshly ground black pepper
3/4	pound veal cutlets, cut into thin 2-inch-long strips
8	ounces ziti
1	medium onion, thinly sliced
1	tablespoon reduced-sodium tomato paste
1	teaspoon minced garlic
1 1/2	cups Sauvignon blanc, *or* other dry white wine
3	cups cauliflower florets
1	teaspoon dried marjoram
2	cups torn Swiss chard leaves

Warm 1 teaspoon oil in a 4-quart pot over medium-high heat for 1 minute. Sprinkle pepper over veal strips, add them to the pot, and sauté until they're lightly browned, about 6 minutes. Transfer strips to a plate, and keep them warm.

Meanwhile, cook pasta according to package directions, omitting salt.

Warm remaining oil in the pot used for sautéing the veal. Add onions and tomato paste; sauté until onions are translucent. Stir in garlic; sauté for 1 minute more.

Return veal to pot. Add wine and cauliflower; simmer mixture until cauliflower is tender, 4 to 5 minutes. Stir in marjoram and chard leaves. Drain pasta; serve stew over it.

HELPFUL HINT

When sautéing the onions and tomato paste, be prepared to lower the heat because tomato paste has a tendency to scorch.

PER SERVING:
Calories: 471
Fat (g): 6.9
Saturated Fat (g): 1.7
Cholesterol (mg): 86
Carbohydrates (g): 53.7
Sodium (mg): 183
Dietary Fiber (g): 6.1

HEARTY ROSEMARY LAMB WITH SWEET POTATOES

The pairing of rosemary and lamb is classic, distinctive, delightful. Here, I offer the two in a robust stew with sweet potatoes and cut green beans.

PREPARATION TIME:

20 minutes

COOKING TIME:

50 minutes

SERVINGS: *4*

2 tablespoons chopped fresh rosemary, *or* 2 teaspoons dried

2 tablespoons chopped fresh thyme, *or* 2 teaspoons dried

1 pound lean lamb shoulder, cut into ¾-inch cubes

1 teaspoon olive oil

1 large onion, cut into thin wedges

3 cups fat-free beef broth

2 bay leaves

1¼ pounds sweet potatoes, peeled and cut into ¾-inch cubes

1½ cups cut green beans

Combine rosemary and thyme. Coat lamb with rosemary-thyme mixture. Warm oil in a 4-quart pot over medium-high heat for 1 minute. Add lamb; sauté until the pieces are lightly browned, about 6 minutes.

Add onions, broth, and bay leaves. Cover pot, and bring mixture to a boil. Reduce heat, and simmer mixture for 30 minutes.

Stir in sweet potatoes and beans; cook vegetables until they're tender, about 10 minutes. Discard bay leaf.

HELPFUL HINT

Using dried rosemary? Then, before adding it to other foods, crush the leaves between your fingers to release their flavor.

PER SERVING:
Calories: 345
Fat (g): 10.4
Saturated Fat (g): 2.9
Cholesterol (mg): 77
Carbohydrates (g): 33.4
Sodium (mg): 249
Dietary Fiber (g): 4.8

LAMB AND TURNIP STEW WITH CILANTRO

This homespun lamb dish has been updated with fresh sage and cilantro. Serve it with crusty bread to sop up the delicious broth.

1 teaspoon olive oil
¾ pound lean lamb shoulder, cut into 1-inch pieces
1 onion, chopped
3 teaspoons minced garlic
½ cup dry red wine
2½ cups low-sodium tomato juice
1 medium potato, cut into ¾-inch cubes
1 large turnip, cut into ¾-inch cubes
1 tablespoon snipped fresh sage, *or* 1 teaspoon dried
½ teaspoon freshly ground black pepper
½ cup snipped fresh cilantro

PREPARATION TIME:
20 minutes
COOKING TIME:
55 minutes
SERVINGS: *4*

Warm oil in a 4-quart pot over medium-high heat for 1 minute. Add lamb and onions; sauté until the lamb pieces are lightly browned and onions are translucent, about 6 minutes.

Add garlic, wine, and 1½ cups juice. Cover pot, and bring mixture to a boil. Reduce heat, and simmer mixture for 25 minutes. Stir in potatoes, turnips, and remaining juice; cook mixture until vegetables are tender, about 20 minutes.

Stir in sage and pepper; cook stew for 1 minute more. Serve stew topped with cilantro.

HELPFUL HINT

To make this stew in your slow cooker: Sauté lamb and onions in a nonstick skillet. Transfer the mixture to an electric slow cooker. Add garlic, wine, 2 cups juice (in this recipe, slow cooking requires less liquid than conventional cooking), potatoes, and turnips. Cover the cooker; cook the stew on Low for 5 to 7 hours. Stir in sage and pepper; cook stew for 10 minutes. Serve stew topped with cilantro.

PER SERVING:
Calories: 298
Fat (g): 7.2
Saturated Fat (g): 2.2
Cholesterol (mg): 74
Carbohydrates (g): 27.5
Sodium (mg): 113
Dietary Fiber (g): 4.8

NEW ENGLAND BOILED DINNER

Never had a home-style New England dinner? Here's a perfect chance to try one. In this version, the meat and vegetables are cut into bite-size morsels for quick cooking. And a mellow maple-mustard sauce smoothes rough-hewn flavors.

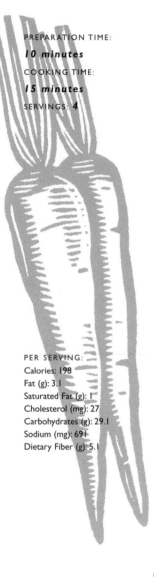

PREPARATION TIME:
10 minutes
COOKING TIME:
15 minutes
SERVINGS: 4

2 tablespoons Dijon mustard

4 tablespoons maple syrup

3 cups fat-free beef broth

1 cup diced turnips

1 cup baby carrots

$\frac{1}{2}$ pound cooked low-sodium smoked ham, cut into $\frac{1}{2}$-inch cubes

1 cup petite Brussels sprouts

1 cup pearl onions

1 teaspoon dried dill weed

$\frac{1}{4}$ teaspoon black pepper

For sauce, combine mustard and syrup in a small glass bowl. Set it aside.

For boiled dinner, combine broth, turnips, and carrots in a 4-quart pot. Cover pot, and bring mixture to a boil. Reduce heat, and simmer mixture for 10 minutes. Add ham, Brussels sprouts, and onions; cook until vegetables are tender, about 5 minutes. Stir in dill weed and pepper. Serve stew with maple-mustard sauce.

HELPFUL HINT

For mild-tasting Brussels sprouts, cook them until they're just crisp-tender.

PER SERVING:
Calories: 198
Fat (g): 3.1
Saturated Fat (g): 1
Cholesterol (mg): 27
Carbohydrates (g): 29.1
Sodium (mg): 691
Dietary Fiber (g): 5.1

LIGHTNING-FAST CHILI

Get Texas-size flavor in this recipe that pairs ground pork and turkey breast with chili beans, fresh tomatoes, and cayenne peppers. Cilantro adds a captivating pungency.

½ pound ground pork
½ pound ground turkey breast
1 cup sliced scallions
1 pound fresh tomatoes, chopped
1 can (15 ounces) chili beans (include the seasonings)
1 yellow cayenne pepper, seeded and chopped
Snipped fresh cilantro, for garnish

In a 4-quart pot over medium-high heat, cook pork and turkey until they're crumbly and no longer pink, about 5 minutes, stirring often and draining off fat as necessary. Add scallions; sauté mixture for 2 minutes more.

Stir in tomatoes, beans, and cayenne pepper. Cover pot, and bring chili to a boil. Reduce heat, and simmer chili for 15 minutes.

HELPFUL HINT

There's a sizable fat difference between ground turkey and ground turkey *breast*. Plain ground turkey contains dark meat as well as skin, so it has much more fat (as well as a more pronounced turkey flavor) than ground breast meat.

PREPARATION TIME:
15 minutes
COOKING TIME:
25 minutes
SERVINGS: *4*

PER SERVING:
Calories: 331
Fat (g): 9.4
Saturated Fat (g): 3.3
Cholesterol (mg): 98
Carbohydrates (g): 27.5
Sodium (mg): 388
Dietary Fiber (g): 7.6

PORK TENDERLOIN WITH GREMOLATA

Often used to flavor up osso buco, an Italian dish made of veal shanks and vegetables, gremolata is a refreshing blend of garlic, lemon peel, and parsley. Here, it perks up a stew of pork, potatoes, and tomatoes.

PREPARATION TIME:
20 minutes
COOKING TIME:
40 minutes
SERVINGS: **4**

1 teaspoon olive oil
¾ pound pork tenderloin, cut into 1-inch pieces
4 shallots, thinly sliced
1 cup fat-free beef broth
2 medium potatoes, cut to ½-inch cubes
1 can (15 ounces) whole tomatoes, cut up
¼ teaspoon freshly ground black pepper
¼ cup gremolata (see Helpful Hint, below)

Warm oil in a 4-quart pot over medium-high heat for 1 minute. Add pork; cook until pieces are lightly browned. Add shallots; sauté mixture until shallots are translucent. Stir in broth; simmer for 10 minutes more.

Stir in potatoes, tomatoes, and black pepper; simmer until potatoes are tender, 15 to 20 minutes. Sprinkle gremolata over each serving.

HELPFUL HINT

Use gremolata to add fresh, sprightly flavor to this and other chowders and stews. Here's how to make it: On a cutting board, mince and blend ¼ cup coarsely snipped parsley, 1 teaspoon lemon peel, and 1 garlic clove.

PER SERVING:
Calories: 271
Fat (g): 5.7
Saturated Fat (g): 1.6
Cholesterol (mg): 67
Carbohydrates (g): 26.9
Sodium (mg): 108
Dietary Fiber (g): 2.7

TENDERLOIN CHILI

Treat your taste buds to high-on-the-hog chili: This super-easy version sports tender, lean pork and fresh tomatoes and has a superb taste that the usual beef chilis can't match.

½ pound cooked pork tenderloin, shredded
1 can (15 ounces) fat-free beef broth
1 pound plum tomatoes, sliced
1 can (14 ounces) pinto beans, rinsed and drained
2 jalapeño peppers, seeded and minced
1 tablespoon chili powder
1 teaspoon cumin seeds, toasted
1 teaspoon Worcestershire sauce

Combine pork, broth, tomatoes, beans, peppers, chili powder, cumin, and Worcestershire sauce in a 3-quart saucepan. Cover the pan, and bring chili to a boil. Reduce heat, and simmer chili for 15 minutes.

HELPFUL HINTS

To toast cumin (or other) seeds, place them in a small nonstick skillet. Warm the seeds over low heat for 5 minutes, shaking the skillet occasionally.

To cook this chili in a slow cooker or a pressure cooker: Combine all ingredients in an electric slow cooker. Cover cooker and cook the chili on Low for 5 hours. Or combine ingredients in a pressure cooker. Lock the cooker's lid into place, and bring cooker up to pressure over medium-high or high heat. Cook chili for 2 minutes, then quick-release the pressure.

PREPARATION TIME:
15 minutes
COOKING TIME:
15 minutes
SERVINGS: **4**

PER SERVING:
Calories: 150
Fat (g): 3.6
Saturated Fat (g): 1
Cholesterol (mg): 45
Carbohydrates (g): 9.9
Sodium (mg): 147
Dietary Fiber (g): 2.8

chili, accomp

chowder, and stew animents

Caraway Wheat Dumplings

Spicy Cheddar Dumplings

Sunflower Dumplings

Dill-Cream Cheese Biscuits

Wheat Biscuits with Poppy Seeds

Garlic Croutons

Crusty Corn Bread

Herbed-Garlic Bread Sticks

Individual Olive Round Breads

Tomato-Basil Focaccia

Dilled Cucumber Salad

Basil Tomatoes

chili, chowder, and stew accompaniments

CARAWAY WHEAT DUMPLINGS

Just as caraway's delicate anise flavor is dominant in rye bread with seeds, it's the standout here. These dumplings will complement almost any hearty stew.

Makes 8 dumplings

PREPARATION TIME:
15 minutes
COOKING TIME:
10 minutes
SERVINGS: *4*

- ¹/₂ cup unbleached flour
- ¹/₂ cup whole wheat flour
- 2 teaspoons baking powder
- ¹/₄ teaspoon salt
- 2 tablespoons butter
- 1 tablespoon caraway seeds
- ¹/₂ cup skim milk

In a medium-size bowl, whisk together flours, baking powder, and salt. Using a pastry blender or two table knives, cut in butter until flour mixture resembles coarse crumbs. Stir in caraway seeds. Pour in milk. Using a fork, mix until ingredients are just combined.

Drop dumplings by the tablespoonsful onto simmering chili, chowder, or stew. Cover pot; cook until dumplings are done, 8 to 10 minutes.

HELPFUL HINTS

A few rules for making light, fluffy dumplings:

Keep stirring to a minimum when you combine the dry ingredients with the liquid. About 10 stirs should do the trick.

Cook dumplings over bubbling hot liquid.

Don't peek—lift the pot lid, to be specific—while dumplings are cooking.

Insert a toothpick or cake tester into the center of a dumpling to see if dumplings are done. If it comes out clean, they are.

PER DUMPLING:
Calories: 181
Fat (g): 6.8
Saturated Fat (g): 3.9
Cholesterol (mg): 17
Carbohydrates (g): 25.6
Sodium (mg): 424
Dietary Fiber (g): 2.5

SPICY CHEDDAR DUMPLINGS

Serve these casual corn-and-hot-pepper-studded breads with any of the robust chilis in this book.

PREPARATION TIME:
15 minutes
COOKING TIME:
10 minutes
SERVINGS: *4*

Makes 8 dumplings

$\frac{1}{2}$ cup cornmeal
$\frac{1}{2}$ cup unbleached flour
 1 teaspoon baking powder
$\frac{1}{2}$ teaspoon crushed red pepper flakes
 2 tablespoons butter
 4 tablespoons shredded extra-sharp Cheddar cheese
 2 tablespoons frozen corn
$\frac{1}{2}$ cup skim milk

In a medium-size bowl, whisk together cornmeal, flour, baking powder, and red pepper. Using a pastry blender or two table knives, cut in butter until flour mixture resembles coarse crumbs. Stir in cheese and corn. Pour in milk. Using a fork, mix until ingredients are just combined.

Drop dumplings by the tablespoonsful onto simmering chili, chowder, or stew. Cover pot; cook until dumplings are done, 8 to 10 minutes.

PER DUMPLING:
Calories: 210
Fat (g): 7.4
Saturated Fat (g): 4.2
Cholesterol (mg): 19
Carbohydrates (g): 28.7
Sodium (mg): 192
Dietary Fiber (g): 1.4

SUNFLOWER DUMPLINGS

A sunflower-packed European-style bread was the inspiration for these nutty-tasting dumplings.

Makes 8 dumplings

- 1 cup unbleached flour
- 2 teaspoons baking powder
- 1/4 teaspoon salt
- 2 tablespoons butter
- 1 tablespoon toasted sunflower seeds
- 1/2 cup skim milk

In a medium-size bowl, whisk together flour, baking powder, and salt. Using a pastry blender or two table knives, cut in butter until flour mixture resembles coarse crumbs. Stir in sunflower seeds. Pour in milk. Using a fork, mix until ingredients are just combined.

Drop dumplings by the tablespoonsful onto simmering chili, chowder, or stew. Cover pot; cook until dumplings are done, 8 to 10 minutes.

PREPARATION TIME:
15 minutes
COOKING TIME:
10 minutes
SERVINGS: *4*

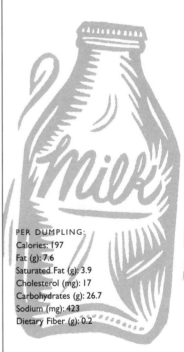

PER DUMPLING:
Calories: 197
Fat (g): 7.6
Saturated Fat (g): 3.9
Cholesterol (mg): 17
Carbohydrates (g): 26.7
Sodium (mg): 423
Dietary Fiber (g): 0.2

DILL-CREAM CHEESE BISCUITS

Fresh dill puts plenty of herbal pizzazz into these tender biscuits. And because they're drop, not roll-'n'-cut, biscuits, they're fast to make.

PREPARATION TIME:
15 minutes
COOKING TIME:
15 minutes

PER BISCUIT:
Calories: 111
Fat (g): 2.9
Saturated Fat (g): 1.6
Cholesterol (mg): 7.3
Carbohydrates (g): 17.5
Sodium (mg): 199
Dietary Fiber (g): 0

Makes 12 biscuits

   Nonstick cooking spray
2 cups unbleached flour
3 teaspoons baking powder
¼ teaspoon salt
2½ tablespoons butter
2½ tablespoons nonfat cream cheese
2 tablespoons finely snipped fresh dill, *or* 2 teaspoons dried
¾ cup skim milk

Coat a baking sheet with spray. Heat oven to 450°.

In a medium-size bowl, whisk together flour, baking powder, and salt. Using a pastry blender or two table knives, cut in butter and cream cheese until flour mixture resembles coarse crumbs. Stir in dill. Pour in milk. Using a fork, mix until ingredients are just combined.

Drop biscuits by the tablespoonsful onto baking sheet. Bake until lightly browned, 10 to 12 minutes. Serve hot.

HELPFUL HINTS

Here are three tips for making sure you've got the most tender, flakiest biscuits around:

Cut in butter while it's cold and hard; warm butter tends to blend with the flour instead of remaining in distinct pieces.

Stir just until the dry and liquid ingredients are combined; about 10 stirs is enough.

Check tops and bottoms of biscuits to see if they're done; both sides should be golden brown.

WHEAT BISCUITS WITH POPPY SEEDS

These slightly nutty-tasting biscuits are as easy as 1-2-3 to make, and they complement any recipe in this book.

Makes 12 biscuits

	Nonstick cooking spray
1½	cups unbleached flour
½	cup whole wheat flour
3	teaspoons baking powder
¼	teaspoon salt
1	tablespoon poppy seeds
3	tablespoons butter
¾	cup skim milk

Coat a baking sheet with spray. Heat oven to 450°.

In a medium-size bowl, whisk together flours, baking powder, salt, and poppy seeds. Using a pastry blender or two table knives, cut in butter until flour mixture resembles coarse crumbs. Pour in milk. Using a fork, mix until ingredients are just combined.

Drop biscuits by the tablespoonsful onto baking sheet. Bake until lightly browned, 10 to 12 minutes. Serve hot.

PREPARATION TIME:

15 minutes

COOKING TIME:

15 minutes

PER BISCUIT:
Calories: 113
Fat (g): 3.7
Saturated Fat (g): 2
Cholesterol (mg): 8.5
Carbohydrates (g): 16.9
Sodium (mg): 188
Dietary Fiber (g): 0.7

GARLIC CROUTONS

Super-simple to make, these croutons make a delightfully crunchy addition to many chilis, chowders, and stews.

PREPARATION TIME:
5 minutes
REFRIGERATION TIME:
10 minutes
SERVINGS: **4**

Makes about 2 cups

4 slices firm whole wheat, *or* white, bread, cut into $\frac{1}{2}$-inch cubes.
Olive oil cooking spray
Garlic powder

Place bread cubes in a large bowl. Mist them with spray and sprinkle them with garlic. Stir cubes and repeat misting them with spray and sprinkling with garlic. Transfer cubes to a baking sheet or a perforated pizza pan.

Broil croutons until they're golden, about 5 minutes. Shake or stir them to expose uncooked sides. Broil croutons until they're golden, about 3 minutes more.

HELPFUL HINTS

Enjoy cheese-garlic croutons? Then sprinkle grated Parmesan or Romano cheese over the bread cubes after dusting them with garlic.

For herbed croutons, sprinkle Italian herb seasoning, garlic, and cheese over the bread cubes.

PER $\frac{1}{2}$ CUP:
Calories: 133
Fat (g): 2.5
Saturated Fat (g): 0.4
Cholesterol (mg): 0
Carbohydrates (g): 24.6
Sodium (mg): 159
Dietary Fiber (g): 2.9

CRUSTY CORN BREAD

Here's an easy machine bread that's perfect for accompanying any chili, chowder, or stew. To make corn bread with a little nip in each bite, add 2 teaspoons red pepper flakes along with the salt and sugar.

Makes 1 loaf (12 slices)

         1   cup water
         1   tablespoon canola oil
         1   tablespoon nonfat milk powder
         1   teaspoon salt
         1   tablespoon sugar
    2 1/2   cups bread flour
       1/2   cup cornmeal
         2   teaspoons bread-machine yeast

Place water, oil, milk, salt, sugar, flour, cornmeal, and yeast in your bread machine pan in the order given. Program machine for a basic white bread; press start. When bread has finished baking, remove it from pan. Let loaf cool on a wire rack.

HELPFUL HINT

This recipe makes a 1 1/2-pound loaf and was tested in a Zojirushi bread machine.

PREPARATION TIME:

10 minutes

COOKING TIME:

4 hours (bread machine)

PER SLICE:
Calories: 142
Fat (g): 1.7
Saturated Fat (g): 0.2
Cholesterol (mg): 0
Carbohydrates (g): 26.7
Sodium (mg): 197
Dietary Fiber (g): 1.3

HERBED-GARLIC BREAD STICKS

Hot, hip, trendy—garlic bread sticks like these come together in no time flat. And no one need know they're made with store-bought frozen dough.

PREPARATION TIME:
15 minutes
(plus 30 minutes resting)
COOKING TIME:
10 minutes

Makes 8 bread sticks

  Olive oil cooking spray
1 tablespoon cornmeal
8 frozen yeast-dough rolls, thawed
$\frac{1}{2}$ teaspoon garlic powder
$\frac{1}{2}$ teaspoon dried marjoram

Coat a baking sheet with spray; dust it with cornmeal.

Stretch and roll each yeast ball into a 12-inch stick; place sticks on baking sheet. Mist them with spray; sprinkle garlic and marjoram over them. Loosely cover the entire sheet with plastic wrap; let sticks rest for 30 minutes in a warm spot. Meanwhile, heat oven to 425°.

Discard plastic wrap. Bake bread sticks until they're golden, about 10 minutes.

HELPFUL HINT

This bread dough acts like a giant elastic band, snapping back into place every time it's stretched. To help keep the bread sticks stretched to a 12-inch length, press the ends of the sticks to the baking sheet.

PER BREAD STICK:
Calories: 109
Fat (g): 2.6
Saturated Fat (g): 0.4
Cholesterol (mg): 9
Carbohydrates (g): 17.9
Sodium (mg): 137
Dietary Fiber (g): 0.7

INDIVIDUAL OLIVE ROUND BREADS

Here, thinly sliced stuffed olives and caramelized onion rings top personal-size focaccia breads.

Makes 8 small breads

Nonstick cooking spray
1 tablespoon cornmeal
8 frozen yeast-dough rolls, thawed
8 stuffed green olives, thinly sliced
½ teaspoon poppy seeds
1 teaspoon olive oil
1 large onion, thinly sliced
1 teaspoon sugar

Coat a baking sheet with spray; dust it with cornmeal.

Gently stretch each roll into a 4-inch circle. Mist top of dough with spray. Arrange olives on dough; sprinkle poppy seeds over dough. Lightly press seasonings into dough.

Warm oil in a large nonstick skillet over medium-high heat for 1 minute. Add onions and sugar; sauté onions until they're wilted and golden, about 6 minutes. Arrange onions on bread rounds.

Loosely cover dough with plastic wrap; let rest for 40 minutes in a warm place. Meanwhile, heat oven to 425°.

Discard plastic wrap. Bake bread rounds until golden brown, 9 to 11 minutes.

HELPFUL HINT

For easiest handling, let the thawed bread dough rise in a warm place for an hour or so before shaping it into rounds.

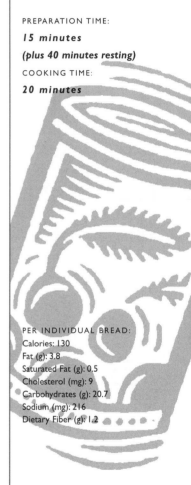

PREPARATION TIME:
15 minutes
(plus 40 minutes resting)
COOKING TIME:
20 minutes

PER INDIVIDUAL BREAD:
Calories: 130
Fat (g): 3.8
Saturated Fat (g): 0.5
Cholesterol (mg): 9
Carbohydrates (g): 20.7
Sodium (mg): 216
Dietary Fiber (g): 1.2

TOMATO-BASIL FOCACCIA

Win rave reviews when you serve this flavorful bread. It's topped with fresh tomatoes, basil, and garlic. Refrigerated dough cuts prep time to practically nothing.

PREPARATION TIME:

20 minutes

COOKING TIME:

15 minutes

Makes 8 slices

    Olive-oil cooking spray
 1 tablespoon cornmeal
 1 package (10 ounces) refrigerated pizza crust
 2 plum tomatoes, thinly sliced
 2 teaspoons minced garlic
10 basil leaves, minced

Heat oven to 425°. Coat a perforated pizza pan with spray; dust it with cornmeal.

Gently stretch dough into a 12-inch circle. Mist top of dough with spray. Arrange tomatoes on dough; sprinkle garlic and basil over tomatoes and dough. Lightly press tomatoes and seasonings into dough.

Bake focaccia until golden brown, 10 to 12 minutes.

HELPFUL HINT

Don't own a perforated pizza pan? Then simply use a rectangular baking sheet and stretch the dough into a large rectangle.

PER SLICE:
Calories: 98
Fat (g): 1.3
Saturated Fat (g): 0.4
Cholesterol (mg): 0
Carbohydrates (g): 18.3
Sodium (mg): 197
Dietary Fiber (g): 2.3

DILLED CUCUMBER SALAD

Dill out! This crisp, cool salad makes a perfect contrasting accompaniment to any robust, nippy chili or stew.

PREPARATION TIME:

15 minutes

SERVINGS: *4*

- ½ cup cider vinegar
- 2 teaspoons olive oil
- 2 tablespoons snipped fresh dill
- 10 grinds black pepper
- 1 teaspoon sugar
- 2 cucumbers, thinly sliced
- 1 medium onion, thinly sliced

For dressing, whisk together vinegar, oil, dill, pepper, and sugar in a small cup.

For salad, combine cucumbers and onions in a medium-size bowl. Pour in dressing; toss until cucumbers are coated with dressing.

HELPFUL HINT

Peel those store-bought cucumbers with waxed skins, but leave the peel on garden-fresh cukes. By not peeling, you'll save time, and you'll add color and crunch to your salad.

PER SERVING:
Calories: 62
Fat (g): 2.5
Saturated Fat (g): 0.4
Cholesterol (mg): 0
Carbohydrates (g): 10.2
Sodium (mg): 5
Dietary Fiber (g): 1.9

BASIL TOMATOES

Here's a refreshing side dish of basil and tomatoes. It's a great go-with for sturdy meat and poultry stews.

PREPARATION TIME:

10 minutes (plus 15 minutes marinating)

SERVINGS: *4*

$\frac{1}{3}$ cup red wine vinegar

2 teaspoons olive oil

$\frac{1}{2}$ teaspoon sugar

2 tablespoons snipped fresh basil

2 tablespoons snipped fresh chives

1 tablespoon snipped fresh parsley

6 grinds black pepper

1 pound tomatoes, thinly sliced

For vinaigrette, whisk vinegar, oil, sugar, basil, chives, parsley, and pepper together in a small bowl. Pour over tomatoes. Let sit 15 minutes before serving.

HELPFUL HINT

Tomatoes pack the most flavor when stored at room temperature. So stash them on the counter, shoulders up, until you're ready to use them.

PER SERVING:
Calories: 47
Fat (g): 2.6
Saturated Fat (g): 0.3
Cholesterol (mg): 0
Carbohydrates (g): 6
Sodium (mg): 11
Dietary Fiber (g): 1.4

appendixes

o n e / g l o s s a r y

Achiote: See *Annatto*.

Adzuki beans: A small dried legume that's especially popular in Japanese cooking. Adzuki beans have a slightly sweet flavor and can be found canned in the ethnic section of many supermarkets.

Allspice: A small, dark-brown berry, this spice tastes like a combination of cinnamon, nutmeg, and cloves; hence, its name. Available whole or ground, allspice flavors both savory and sweet dishes.

Anaheim peppers: See *Peppers*.

Ancho peppers: See *Peppers*.

Annatto: Often used to color cheese and margarine, annatto lends subtle flavor and orange-yellow color to many Latin American dishes. To use annatto, which is sold as whole seeds (and may be known as *achiote seeds*), sauté the seeds in oil, remove them with a slotted spoon, then use the flavorful colored oil to sauté onions or meats. Or grind the seeds, using a mortar and pestle, and add the powder to dishes as they simmer. Look for annatto seeds with a rusty color; brown ones are past their prime.

Bay leaf: May also be called *bay laurel* or *laurel leaf*. This herb, which is rarely available fresh, is a standard component of bouquet garni and pickling spice and provides subtle flavor to soups, stews, and other saucy dishes. Look for it dried in most supermarkets. And always discard it at the end of cooking.

Bell peppers: See *Peppers*.

Black-eyed peas: Sometimes called a *cowpea*, this small, beige legume has an oval black "eye" at the center of its curve. Its flavor is earthy; its texture, mealy. Look for black-eyed peas fresh, frozen, canned, or dried; they're available in most supermarkets.

Blanch: To cook fruits or vegetables partially by dipping them into boiling water or by steaming them briefly ($\frac{1}{2}$ to 2 minutes), then plunging them into icy water to stop the cooking process. Why blanch? To set flavor and color or to loosen skins.

Cacciatore: In Italian, "cacciatore" means prepared "hunter-style." This Italian-American dish is typically made with mushrooms, onions, tomatoes, herbs, chicken, and, sometimes, red wine.

Cannellini: Large white kidney beans popular in many Italian soups and salads. You can find them canned and dried in most supermarkets.

Cayenne peppers: See *Peppers*.

Chili: A Tex-Mex dish often called *a bowl of red* or *chili con carne*, which means "chile with meat" in Spanish. An alternate spelling for "chili" is *chile*. The origins of this well-seasoned dish are controversial and discussions of its ingredients can evoke intense arguments. Texans consider it a crime to add beans to "a bowl of red," while cooks in other areas of the U.S. routinely include beans, especially red kidney beans. Most chili recipes call for chili peppers or chili powder.

Chili powder: A spicy blend of six dried and ground seasonings: chili peppers, oregano, cumin, garlic, coriander, and cloves. Chili powder provides the intense, characteristic flavors found in chilis and other popular Mexican- and Tex-Mex-style dishes. It's available in the spice aisle of most supermarkets.

Chinese five-spice powder: True to its name, this seasoning has just five spices usually in equal parts: Cinnamon, cloves, fennel seed, star anise, and Szechuan peppers. Look for it in the spice aisle of your supermarket, and use it to flavor up Asian-style stir-fries and stews.

Chinese wheat noodles: These fast-cooking, extremely thin noodles are made from wheat, water, salt, and, occasionally, eggs. Their flavor is delicate and nutty. Look for them in your supermarket's ethnic aisle. If you can't find them, substitute extra-thin spaghetti or angel-hair pasta.

Chowder: This is a thick, chunky soup. Clam and other seafood chowders are the most well-known. Common bases for chowders include cream-style corn, milk, and tomatoes.

Cilantro: Also called *Chinese parsley*, *Mexican parsley*, and *fresh coriander*. Cilantro refers to the bright green, delicate-looking leaves of the coriander plant. Its scent is often described as musty, and its flavor is distinctive and entirely different from that of coriander seeds, which also come from the coriander plant. When buying this herb, a seasoning used extensively in Mexican, Caribbean, and Asian cooking, look for bunches of perky green leaves. Store cilantro for up to a week in the refrigerator in a plastic bag. Wash the leaves just before using them.

Coriander: A small tan seed that tastes like a blend of lemon, sage, and caraway.

Corned beef: Cured beef brisket or round with a deep red color and a somewhat salty taste. You can find cooked corned beef in your supermarket's deli case and ready-to-cook beef in the meat section. Canned, cooked corned beef is also available.

Couscous: A quick-cooking pasta—it takes just 5 minutes to prepare—couscous is a staple in numerous North African cuisines. Look for this tasty alternative to rice in your supermarket's ethnic aisle. Couscous is also the name of a delicious entrée in which cracked wheat is steamed over a simmering stew of chicken, raisins, chick peas, and spices in a special pot called a couscousière.

Cream-style corn: Though creamy in appearance, there's nary a drop of the dairy stuff in this corn product. When commercially prepared, cream-style corn contains corn, sugar, and cornstarch. The homemade version is nothing more than the pulp and juice squeezed from corn kernels.

Cubanel pepper: See *Peppers*.

Dredge: To coat a food, such as pieces of chicken, with a dry ingredient, such as flour or cornmeal. Dredging can add flavor and help browning.

Focaccia: An Italian yeast bread similar to pizza. The bread is usually brushed with olive oil, then topped with thinly sliced vegetables, such as olives, onions, and tomatoes.

Gingerroot: This is the gnarled, knobby root of a tropical and subtropical plant. Its aroma is pungent and spicy; its flavor, sweet and peppery. A signature seasoning in many Asian and East Indian dishes, gingerroot has a thin tan skin, which should be removed before using, and pale yellowish flesh. Look for this flavorful root in your supermarket's produce section, and choose one with a smooth skin; wrinkling indicates a dry oldster. Gingerroot will keep on your counter for several days. Or peel it, cut it into 1-inch chunks, and freeze it in a self-sealing plastic bag for up to 6 months. A 1-inch piece equals about 1 tablespoon when minced. The powdered, dried version has a markedly different flavor and is most often used in baked goods, such as gingersnaps.

Gremolata: Sometimes spelled *gremolada*. Freshly minced parsley, grated lemon peel, and minced garlic make up this sprightly seasoning that's usually sprinkled over osso bucco and other stews.

Gruyère cheese: A wonderfully nutty, slightly assertive cheese with small holes and an ivory color. Gruyère's flavor rivals that of Swiss cheese, and the two are often used interchangeably in dishes such as sauces, quiches, and fondues. Processed Gruyère contains both Emmentaler (a type of Swiss cheese) and Gruyère and has a flavor that's noticeably different from that of natural Gruyère.

Gumbo: A Creole specialty of New Orleans, gumbo is thick with seafood, meat, poultry, sausage, and vegetables, including tomatoes, onions, and—a Louisiana favorite—okra. It's usually made with a rich flour and butter roux and is traditionally thickened with okra as well as filé powder, a tricky-to-use seasoning that easily gets stringy and tough. Gumbo comes from an African word for okra.

Habanero pepper: See *Peppers*.

Herbs: See *Appendix Five* for combinations with foods.

Herbes de Provence: A traditional blend of six dried herbs—rosemary, marjoram, thyme, sage, anise seed, and savory—that's typical of the cuisine of southern France. Use it to season chicken, pork, veal, fish, and shrimp.

Hickory smoke flavoring: See *Smoke flavoring*.

Hot-pepper sauce: One of numerous Louisiana-style sauces made with hot chili peppers, vinegar, and salt. The flavor and heat vary from brand to brand, some being relatively mild; others, are so scorching that a single drop fires up an entire chili or stew. When using a hot sauce for the first time, cautiously add it to dishes, tasting the results after each drop.

Instant flour: A specially formulated flour that dissolves quickly—and with minimal lumping—in hot or cold liquids. It's used primarily for thickening sauces and gravies.

Italian herb seasoning: This is a delightful herb blend of basil, oregano, and thyme; occasionally garlic powder, red pepper, and rosemary are included. Use the mix to give entrées and side dishes characteristic Italian flavor.

Jalapeño pepper: See *Peppers*.

Kielbasa: Also labeled *kielbasy*, this is a robust smoked Polish sausage that's mostly available precooked, but for best flavor, it's served hot. Traditional kielbasa contains pork and spices, but beef may be added. Newer turkey versions have less fat.

Lemon pepper: A seasoning blend of grated lemon peel, or zest, and black pepper. Read the label before buying this blend; some brands contain more salt than pepper or lemon.

Lentils: Meaty tasting and packed with protein, lentils are small disk-shaped legumes that come in three varieties: Grayish-brown (European), reddish-orange (Egyptian), and yellow. Of the three, the grayish-brown are most often found in supermarkets; the other types can be obtained in Middle Eastern and Indian groceries. Stored at room temperature in a dry place, lentils will keep for a year.

Marjoram: This delightful herb, a member of the mint family, is also called *sweet marjoram*. It has long, oval gray-green leaves and a very mild oregano-like flavor. To retain its delicate taste, add it to dishes toward the end of the cooking.

Mesquite flavoring: See *Smoke flavoring*.

Mortar and pestle: A simple kitchen tool consisting of bowl (mortar) and a small bat-shaped cylinder (pestle). A mortar and pestle set is used to crush or grind spices, seeds, and dried herbs. Most sets are made from porcelain, metal, or wood; a few—those with designer prices—are made from marble.

Mushrooms: Not a single food, but an intriguing family of wild and cultivated edible fungi that range in texture from delicate to meaty and in flavor from mild to nutty. Colors include white, golden, and brown. When buying mushrooms, select those that are plump, firm, and fresh looking. To clean them, wipe them with a damp towel or gently rinse them in cool water. Never soak fresh mushrooms; too much water dilutes and ruins their flavor. These are three popular and readily available varieties:

Common or Button: White in color (occasionally brown), these mild-flavored, small mushrooms range in size from $\frac{1}{2}$ inch to 3 inches in diameter. Look for their familiar umbrella shape.

Portobello: These huge brown mushrooms—caps often measure as much as 6 inches across—are the mature relatives of the common, cultivated variety. Their texture is meaty and flavor, earthy. Creative ways to use these spectacular fungi: Grilled whole caps in sandwiches; marinated, grilled whole caps as side dishes; thickly sliced and sautéed in salads and entrées; chopped and sautéed in soups and stews.

Shiitake: Brown in color (occasionally with tan striations), a shiitake mushroom has these characteristics: A large floppy cap that's anywhere from 2 to 10 inches across; a tough, slender stem that's usually discarded; and a full-bodied flavor that some connoisseurs say is steak-like. Once available only in Asian groceries, shiitake mushrooms can now be found in most large supermarkets but tend to be pricey.

Okra: This green vegetable has a ridged, oblong, tapered shape and a mild, asparagus-like flavor. When cooked, it develops a ropy, or slippery, quality that thickens the cooking liquid. Look for crisp, brightly colored, blemish-free pods that are shorter than 4 inches long. Large pods are oldies and may be tough and fibrous.

Peppers, sweet and hot: Crisp, colorful, flavorful, mild, hot, versatile, high in vitamin C, a good source of vitamin A, readily available—such attributes make peppers a favored vegetable in many cuisines: Chinese, Hungarian, Mexican, Thai, to name a few. Though there are tons of pepper varieties, all can be divided into two basic categories—sweet and hot. Here's a quick rundown of several popular and easily obtained varieties:

Anaheim: A long, slender, moderately hot pepper (chili) that's also known as *New Mexican, long green, long red,* or *California.* They're the pepper of choice in the classic Mexican dish, chiles rellenos.

Ancho: A dried poblano chili that's 3 to 4 inches long, has a reddish-brown color, and a mild to pungent flavor. The name means "wide chili" in Spanish.

Bell: A sweet, bell-shaped pepper that ranges in size from medium to very large and comes in several colors: Green, red, yellow, orange, brown, and purple. These peppers, often called *sweet peppers,* are suitable for roasting, stuffing, slicing, dicing, and pureeing. Use them to add crunch, color, and flavor in just about any chili, casserole, or stew.

Cayenne: A long, thin, sharply pointed hot pepper that's either straight or curled. Generally, cayennes are sold when fully ripe and red in color. They're also available dried.

Cubanel: A long (about 4 inches from tip to core), tapered pepper that's also known as an *Italian frying pepper* (and often spelled *cubanelle*). The peppers come in light green or yellow and are perfectly suited to sautéing.

Habanero: An extremely hot, small, orange-yellow chili. In Jamaica, it's known as *Scotch bonnet.* Because these peppers have so much firepower (200,000–300,000 Scoville Units, a relative heat measurement), you'll want to use them sparingly.

Jalapeño: A tapered, 2-inch-long, very hot pepper that's usually sold at the green, but mature, stage. These peppers are used to season cheese, jellies, and sausage and are the most widely consumed chili in the United States.

Pimiento: A large, red, heart-shaped mild pepper that's usually sold in jars. Thick and meaty, pimientos (sometimes spelled *pimentos*) are ideal for roasting, if you can find them fresh.

Poblano: A very dark green, moderately hot pepper that resembles a stubby bell pepper with a tapered blossom end.

Serrano: A long, slender, very hot pepper that is usually sold green and often used in fresh salsas.

Picante sauce: A tomato-based condiment that's smoother than a salsa but has a similar flavor. Spiciness ranges from mild to mouth-searing.

Pigeon pea: A grayish-yellow pea (originally hailing from Africa) that's popular in the southern United States. Pigeon peas are available canned, fresh, frozen, and dried.

Pimiento: See *Peppers.*

Poblano pepper: See *Peppers.*

Pork tenderloin: This is an extremely lean pork loin roast cut from the hog's back. When cooked, the meat is tender and white with clear juices. Tasty ways with this cut include roasting, stir-frying, sautéing, and grilling as well as stewing.

Portobello: See *Mushrooms.*

Ratatouille: A traditional dish from France's Provençal region, ratatouille usually combines eggplant, tomatoes, onions, bell peppers, zucchini, garlic, and seasonings. Serve it hot, cold, or at room temperature.

Refried beans: This high-fiber, tasty Mexican specialty is made from red beans or pinto beans that are cooked, seasoned, mashed, and then fried in lard. Today, canned varieties are available in low-fat and fat-free styles. Also known and labeled as *frijoles refritos* and *refritos*.

Roman beans: Often called *cranberry beans*, these delicious legumes are small, oval, and tan-colored with specks and streaks of burgundy. Roman beans are available canned and dried in most supermarkets. Roman bean math: 1 pound dried equals 7 cups cooked.

Romano cheese: A light yellow cheese with a nippy flavor and hard texture similar to that of Parmesan cheese. The two cheeses are generally grated, often added to Italian-style dishes, and may be interchanged in recipes. For maximum flavor, use freshly grated cheese.

Rosemary: Cooks often describe the taste of this aromatic herb as piny. That's not surprising since its narrow green leaves resemble pine needles. Before using the leaves, chop the fresh variety and crush the dried form in a mortar and pestle or between your fingers. Rosemary is fairly assertive, especially when fresh, so apply it with restraint.

Sage: Sporting grayish-green leaves, which have a soft velvet-like surface, sage is an herb native to the Mediterranean. Its flavor stands out, pleasantly so, in traditional sausage mixes as well as poultry stuffings. When buying fresh sage, look for bunches of leaves with no blemishes or wilting. Keep sage, unwashed, in a plastic bag in the refrigerator for up to 4 days. Dried sage comes whole, rubbed (crumbled), and ground. Feel free to interchange rubbed and ground varieties in recipes. And because dried sage loses its spunk within about 3 months, get it in small quantities.

Sancoche: A hearty Latin American stew of meat, fish, vegetables, and seasonings.

Savory: A somewhat assertive herb that's a cousin to mint and comes in two varieties: Winter and summer. Of the two, the winter variety has a stronger minty-thyme flavor. Look for savory fresh or dried.

Serrano pepper: See *Peppers*.

Shallot: Even though related to onions, shallots resemble giant, brown garlic bulbs. Each bulb is composed of multiple cloves, each covered with a thin, papery skin. Select shallots that are plump and firm with no signs of wilting, sprouting, or mold. And keep them in a cool, dry spot for up to a month. Prepare and use shallots, which are mild in flavor, in the same manner as onions.

Shiitake: See *Mushrooms*.

Smoke flavoring: Available in liquid form, smoke flavoring is nothing more than smoke concentrate in a water base. Popular flavors include hickory and mesquite. Use it to add a new dimension to chilis, sauces, and stews.

Snow peas: These delicate peas have bright-green, thin edible pods, and the French call them *mange-tout*, to "eat it all." Select crisp, well-colored pods with small peas. To store them, place in a plastic bag for up to three days. Pinch off the ends before using them. Sometimes called *Chinese snow peas*.

Sofrito: This flavorful, thick sauce is used as a seasoning in many Spanish and Caribbean recipes. It's traditionally made with annatto seeds, pork (or rendered pork fat), onions, sweet peppers, garlic, and herbs and is available in jars in the international section of many large supermarkets. Just a tablespoon or two will pump up any stew that needs a little special character.

Spices: See *Appendix Five* for combinations with foods.

Stew: Any dish in which the ingredients—usually meat, poultry, fish, and vegetables—have been simmered, or stewed, in a liquid until they're tender. Stews may be cooked either on the stove top or in the oven in a covered vessel. The difference between a stew and hearty soup is slight: Stews usually have larger pieces of food, and the liquid is often thickened before serving.

Teriyaki: A delightful homemade or commercially prepared sauce made of soy sauce, sake (or sherry), sugar, ginger, and garlic. Popular uses for teriyaki, which has a Japanese origin, include marinating beef, poultry, and seafood for broiling, grilling, or stir-frying. The term "teriyaki" also refers to any dish made with a teriyaki sauce.

Thai spice: This is an exotic blend of spices—chili peppers, ginger, coriander, cumin, cinnamon, star anise, garlic, lemon peel, and dried shallots—and may be labeled *Thai seasoning*. It imparts robust, warm flavor to noodles, rice, stews, and other dishes. Thai spice can be found in the spice aisle of most supermarkets.

Tomatillo: A signature ingredient in salsa verde, the tomatillo is a small green fruit that's covered by a thin, papery, brown husk. The fruit has flavor hints of lemon, apples, and spices and is often used in Mexican and Tex-Mex foods. Choose tomatillos with tight-fitting, dry husks and no signs of mold. Store tomatillos in a paper bag in the refrigerator for up to a month. Before using these somewhat tart fruits, remove and discard the husks and wash the fruit.

Tortilla: Made from corn (called *masa*) or wheat flour, tortillas are thin, flat, round, unleavened Mexican breads that resemble slender pancakes. Traditionally, tortillas are baked, but not browned, on a griddle. They can be eaten plain or wrapped around a multitude of fillings to create tacos, burritos, enchiladas, tostadas, and chimichangas. Pick up packaged tortillas in your supermarket's refrigerator section; store them according to package directions.

Vegetable protein crumbles: May also be labeled *soy vegetable crumbles*. Created as a meatless alternative to ground beef, these tasty, low-fat (but often high-sodium) products are made with soy protein and seasonings. You can find them in the frozen-food section of most supermarkets.

Wild rice: Sometimes called *Indian rice* or *Canadian rice*, this chewy, nutty-tasting food isn't rice at all but the dark-brown seed of a tall marsh grass. It's the only cereal grain native to North America. Uncooked wild rice will keep indefinitely when stored in a tightly closed container in a cool dry place or in a refrigerator. Since wild rice may contain debris collected during harvesting and processing, wash it before cooking. Simply place the rice in a pan of cool water and let it soak for a minute or so; unwanted particles will float to the top where they can be removed.

Worcestershire sauce: A widely available, commercially made dark, pungent condiment. The exact ingredients in this tasty sauce are a trade secret, but food experts agree that these are the basics: Soy sauce, vinegar, garlic, tamarind, onions, molasses, lime, and anchovies. Worcestershire sauce was first concocted in India and bottled in Worcestershire, England; hence, its name. It's ideal for perking up chilis, chowders, stews, soups, meats, gravies, and vegetable juices.

Yukon gold potatoes: These are one of several varieties of thin-skinned potatoes with a buttery yellow flesh. Their flavor is mildly buttery as well. Tasty uses include baking and boiling for casseroles, soups, and stews.

two/kitchen calculations

Think quick, now. A chowder recipe requires 1 cup of broccoli florets. How many pounds of fresh broccoli or how many packages of frozen should you buy? A stew takes 2 cups of fat-free chicken broth. How many cans of broth should you open? Uncertain? Don't worry; you're not alone. To help you (me, and others) out, I've listed approximate equivalents (it's impossible to be exact) in the following tables.

Dairy

Butter: 1 stick = $\frac{1}{4}$ pound = 4 ounces = 8 tablespoons
Cheese, blue, feta, Gorgonzola: 4 ounces = 1 cup crumbled
Cheese, Cheddar, Monterey Jack: 1 pound = 4 cups shredded or grated
Cheese, Parmesan, Romano: 4 ounces = 1 cup shredded or grated
Cream, half & half, sour: $\frac{1}{2}$ pint = 1 cup